Values into Practice in Special Education

Edited by

Geoff Lindsay
David Thompson

David Fulton Publishers
London

David Fulton Publishers Ltd
Ormond House, 26–27 Boswell Street, London WC1N 3JD

First published in Great Britain by David Fulton Publishers 1997

Note: The right of Geoff Lindsay and David Thompson to be identified as the editors of this work has been asserted by them in accordance with the Copyright, Designs and Patents Act 1988.

Copyright © David Fulton Publishers Ltd 1997

British Library Cataloguing in Publication Data
A catalogue record for this book is available from the British Library

ISBN 1–85346–466–X

Typeset by FSH Print and Production, London
Printed in Great Britain by BPC Books and Journals, Exeter

Contents

Foreword

Klaus Wedell

A book about values might at first not strike practitioners in special needs as immediately relevant to their everyday concerns. But you only have to listen for a moment to what they and parents talk about, to notice that in fact concern about values lies at the root of many of their dilemmas. A while ago a Special Needs Coordinator said to me: 'You'd think that the recent education legislation was designed to make it difficult for us to collaborate with other schools in meeting pupils' special educational needs.'

This comment is just one illustration of the concerns about values which have become more prevalent as the current market economy policies impact on education. Another instance is the way that the Parent's Charter seems to present the Statement procedure as offering a right to open-ended resourcing for their children. It is obvious that, at a time of constraints, such a view is unlikely to be endorsed in any community's values. A further example is teachers' daily dilemma about pressing ahead with the National Curriculum Programmes of Study while worrying about the proportion of their pupils who are being left behind.

This book will therefore make a contribution by bringing into the open the conflicting values which often lie behind the decisions which teachers and others involved in special needs education have to make. Many will have been aware of the dilemmas about values in their daily experience, but not in an explicit way. Others may just have been aware of the stress which the dilemmas have occasioned but not recognised the dilemmas themselves. It is hardly surprising that there has been a marked increase in the proportion of early retirements due to illness among teachers in recent years. By helping readers to acknowledge the issue of values, this book will enable many to realise what may have been worrying them. They will recognise where the conflicts and dilemmas lie. There may also be some who have not experienced dilemmas because they have been unaware of values other than their own. For these practitioners the book will hopefully open up a new perspective which will enhance their practical effectiveness.

It is well known that much of the conflict between parents of children with special educational needs and the professionals serving them arises from unrecognised discrepancies in the value perceptions of both parties. By revealing the source of these conflicts this book will hopefully lead to a better understanding of each other. The chapter on the development of children's values may well prove to be revealing for parents and practitioners alike.

The editors and contributors to this book are in a good position to write on this topic, since they have all been involved in it at a practical as well as theoretical level. Furthermore, some have been working to establish the values they write about. It will soon be very apparent to readers that, far from dealing with an obscure set of notions, this book in fact addresses their day-to-day concerns. Indeed, they will come to wonder why such a book has not appeared before!

Klaus Wedell
May 1997

Editors' Note

The time of editing and writing this book coincided with a period of our lives which was challenging for both of us, and highlighted the need to be clear about what is of real value.

Notes on Authors

Derrick Armstrong is a Senior Lecturer in the Division of Education, University of Sheffield.

Roger Attwood is Senior Educational Psychologist, Psychological Service, Sheffield LEA.

Robert Burden is Reader in Educational Psychology, School of Education, University of Exeter.

Martin Desforges is Senior Educational Psychologist, Psychological Services, Sheffield LEA and Associate Tutor, Division of Education, University of Sheffield.

Julie Dockrell is Senior Lecturer, Child Development and Learning, Institute of Education, London.

Geoff Lindsay is Professor in Special Needs Education and Educational Psychology, and Director of the Special Needs Research Unit, Institute of Education, University of Warwick.

Ingrid Lunt is Reader in Psychology and Special Needs, Institute of Education, London.

Sonia Sharp is Principal Educational Psychologist, Buckinghamshire.

David Thompson is Senior Lecturer, Division of Education, University of Sheffield.

Klaus Wedell is Emeritus Professor, Institute of Education, London.

Part 1

Values in the Wider Community

Chapter 1

Values and Special Education

Geoff Lindsay and David Thompson

The world of special education is diverse, comprising those professionals, families and administrators who find themselves working together to meet children's needs. Behind them is another world – the world of central government, civil servants, and the great British Public who give the political will to the system. These worlds interact over long periods of time, sometimes with consensus, but on other occasions different participants are in conflict. Everyone's intention is to support the children, but how do we weigh the costs and benefits of the changes that occur in the lives of the children themselves, their families and the others with whom they interact? How do we balance concern for the child with special needs against the needs of other children in a class, school or wider community? How do we reconcile differential levels of provision?

These judgements are influenced by the main interests and values of those concerned, with overlaps but also distinctions within and between groups. For example, the parents will share many similar values to those held by parents of children without special needs; parents as a whole will also differ in their values as a result of their various religious and secular moral beliefs. An individual teacher's views will show similar characteristics compared with those of other teachers, and there will also be overlap with parents' views. But a teacher has different experiences and responsibilities and hence may have different priorities when judging particular issues.

Educational values have been defined as values to which we appeal in judging the worth of actions, programmes and products which are, or claim to be, conducive to the education of the child (Ormell 1980). In other words, they are principles or beliefs held by individuals, either by themselves or by group membership, which are used as criteria for making judgements on preferred courses of action. Some authors use the word 'value' as a verb: individuals value certain actions or principles they see as important, and having a high priority on time and resources (Barrow 1975; Holmes and Lindley 1991).

Although we tend to separate 'facts' from 'values', in reality such a distinction is problematic. Certain approaches to research emphasise the former and stress the need for objectivity, but there is criticism of this notion of 'value-free' science (Lindsay 1995a). For example, while certain evidence may indeed be objective, the decision to choose those particular data, those subjects, and even undertake the study in question rather than another, are all influenced by value judgements. The decisions to undertake research into provision for children with special educational needs (SEN), how much to allocate, and which programmes to support are influenced both by factual and value considerations. The same applies to the dissemination, or not, of the outcomes of such research, with some government agencies, for example, refusing to guarantee a proper freedom to researchers they contract to publish their findings.

Similarly, decisions regarding provision as a whole in a school or local education authority (LEA), and those with respect to individual children, are influenced both by the facts and by value judgements. Indeed, the latter can influence how 'facts' are presented, which to include, to emphasise or to leave out. Hence the values held by the participants can heavily influence the factual description of the situation. Knowledge of their own values, where they arise from and how they relate to their personal identity can therefore be important in enabling them to work with others to achieve an effective decision which genuinely meets the best interests of the child.

What is the current situation here in the UK in the late 1990s? What values are embedded in the ways of describing children's difficulties, and to what extent are these legacies from the past? What values determine legislation, and the procedures and rights derived therefrom? Indeed, what values do we hold for children with special educational needs?

Do we value children with special educational needs?

There has been a major programme of legislation whose aim has been to improve the system of education for children with special educational needs – see Chapter 2. Together with other legislation, such as the Children Act 1989, the statutory framework now appears to provide much greater safeguards. Consequently, the answer to the question posed above appears to be obvious: we must value children with SEN otherwise why would we go to the trouble to legislate for their well-being? But is this so? A closer examination reveals a more complex scenario, for at the same time other legislation was being introduced.

League tables

One of the Conservative government's avowed aims was to improve standards in schools (see Chapter 2). However, we must ask – standards of what, and for what? The publication of the first set of primary league tables of Key Stage 2 results provides an interesting reflection. These results received widespread coverage in the media, and were promoted by the Secretary of State, Gillian

Shephard, as providing useful information. However, critics have argued that the raw data do not allow a fair analysis of the contribution of schools serving disadvantaged areas, or those with many children with SEN. Proponents of the 'value added' approach to school measurement recommend that the data be re-analysed taking such factors into account. Where this has occurred, schools and LEAs have been found to change their relative positions on the table, sometimes alarmingly. This practice is sound in principle, although the technical problems are usually under-estimated (e.g. Lindsay 1995a). Note also that the purpose is to remove children with SEN to allow a 'fair' judgement of the school. Furthermore, many lauded the achievements of the small group of schools which achieved 100 per cent of their children achieving Level 4.

But here we see some major conflicts. Take a school which would have achieved 100 per cent if its five pupils with severe and complex difficulties had been excluded from the calculation. But suppose that these children had made equally impressive achievements in their own terms. How will this be captured if they are excluded? What does this indicate for the value we place on their achievements, to treat them here as irritants in the analysis? And should we praise schools with 100 per cent results anyway, if this indicates they are not inclusive of children with SEN?

Selection

Parents, in theory, now have the right to choose, but evidence is accruing that it is schools which select, but not all schools. Rather, some schools, those which are popular and over-subscribed may select to become even more homogeneous, and it is proposed that this previously secondary phenomenon be encouraged in primary schools. How many schools will actively seek children with special educational needs? Even parents of apparently able children are having a rough ride if Frances Beckett is representative (*Guardian Education*, 18 March 1997). In her article 'Battered and bruised we held our breath ...' she concludes: 'It is a most remarkable example of Orwellian Doublespeak that this misery has been imposed on families in the name of parental choice.' (p.3).

Do systems such as these indicate valuing of children as a whole and, more particularly, those with SEN? Or, rather, is it not the case that these children are seen as irritants, variables to be used to modify data, or 'unfortunate' casualties of a system designed to ensure that those who are most favoured receive the best?

Effects of social policies on health

Consider also what the data on children's health indicate for the values we hold about their welfare. In many respects this has been a success story. Infant mortality rates have dropped considerably since the nineteenth century, across all countries in the developed world. Within the UK they have reduced across all regions and all social classes. However, as Spencer (1996) shows, there remain *differentials* in infant mortality between regions and class. Also, these differentials can be demonstrated for childhood illnesses and other child health issues. For example, if we compare rates of occurrence for children in the Registrar General's Social Class V (lowest) with Social Class (highest), we find that they are:

• twice as likely to die after infancy
• seven times as likely to die in road traffic accidents
• eight times as likely to die in a fire
• and children in the most deprived ten per cent of local authority electoral wards were 15 times as likely to die from a head injury as children in the least deprived 10 per cent (Spencer 1996).

Furthermore, the same pattern of inequality can be shown for low birth weight, failure to thrive, incidence of cerebral palsy, respiratory infections, otitis media (middle ear infections with temporary, but often sustained, hearing loss) and many other illnesses, as well as behaviour problems, and poorer educational outcomes. In addition, Spencer argues that child poverty in the USA and UK has recently risen dramatically. In the UK, for example, the rate has changed from 9% around 1980 to 31% in 1992.

There have now been many studies which have demonstrated significant health inequalities relative to social class and degrees of poverty, and Spencer's is an excellent summary of this field. The conclusions to be drawn are that governments, not only in the UK, have not placed high priority on children in general, let alone those children who have disabilities or special educational needs. The dominant philosophy in the UK and USA during the 1980s and early 1990s has been that of 'personal responsibility'. In the case of health, the focus has been away from general, pervasive influences amply shown to affect health outcomes, and instead to concentrate on individual responsibility for health: cutting down smoking; not engaging in unsafe sex; maintaining a healthy weight; etc. Now, all of these are important, and personal responsibility is a key element, but an historical analysis of health promotion indicates that the most powerful impact has been made by public health measures (e.g. water purity, improved housing, mass immunisation) rather than individual actions. Spencer (1996) argues: 'Neo-liberal, monetarist economic and social policies pursued in developed countries such as the UK and the USA in recent years have been responsible for increasing child poverty and exacerbating its health consequences.' (p.207)

Models of disability and special needs

Traditionally children with learning, physical and sensory difficulties were conceptualised within a model which focused on their own hypothetical deficiencies. This has often been called the 'deficiency', 'within child' or 'medical' model. Indeed, these terms often appear to be used interchangeably, although there are subtle distinctions.

Deficiency

The child's abilities in one domain (e.g. cognition) are considered to be below a particular level *and* the actual level is considered to be lower than that required for satisfactory development. Note that there are two aspects of this approach. The first is essentially a measurement issue: what is the cut-off point? The second is functional: deficiency in music alone is not considered a major problem, deficiency in reading or general cognitive ability is.

Within child

The focus of causation of the difficulties is clearly within the child. This may be based on physical evidence (e.g. profound hearing loss, cerebral palsy), an hypothesis based on functioning (e.g. low levels of reading ability), or on difficulties in abilities considered to be pre-requisite for skill development (e.g. the child is not reading because he or she is considered to have poorly developed perceptual or phonological skills). External factors (e.g. quality of teaching) are not considered as a direct causation.

Medical model

This term is often used in a confusing manner, confounding different notions of a medical model. In the present context, the implication is that the causation is physical (e.g. constitutional, genetic, result of an accident). It is thus very similar to the 'within child' model. However, confusion often exists as the term 'medical model' is also used to describe practice where medical personnel are dominant and 'in charge'. Even if there is a multi-disciplinary team the medical member (e.g. paediatrician in a paediatric assessment team, psychiatrist in a child guidance team) may be ultimately responsible, and their conceptual framework may dominate.

Since the 1970s in particular alternative models have been in vogue. The two main approaches are the 'needs' and 'social' models.

Needs model

The Warnock Report (DES 1978) introduced into official government discourse the term *special educational needs*. This promoted a focus on the needs of the child rather than the origin or causation of the difficulties. However, inherent in this, and indeed to a large extent as a result of earlier debate within the educational psychology literature (e.g. Gillham 1978), is the concept of *interaction*. A child's learning difficulties must be seen as a result of an interaction of various factors including their own strengths and weaknesses which may be the result of constitutional or experiential factors, and the influence of the environment, in particular the school and family.

Needs are specified relative to the child's present status and the future goals determined by key people – parents, professionals, the children themselves. In this model, needs can be of two kinds: future status and means to achieve this. For example, a child with very poor writing skills (whether the result of athetoid cerebral palsy, limited sight vocabulary or inefficient teaching) may be considered to 'need' to achieve a particular level of competence, relative to age-related expectation. But the term may also refer to what is necessary in order to achieve this goal: the child may 'need' a particular writing programme or a piece of IT equipment.

Social model

The preceding models have largely been determined by professionals and applied to children (and adults) with disabilities or special needs. With increasing power as their numbers and influence swell, alternative models have been proposed by the people previously the subject of such definition. Barnes (1996) describes this socio-political approach thus:

> a growing number of academics, many of whom are disabled people themselves, have re-conceptualised disability as a complex and sophisticated form of social oppression... or institutional discrimination on a par with sexism, hetrosexism and racism... theoretical analysis has shifted from individuals and their impairment to disabling environments and hostile social attitudes. (Barnes 1996, p.1)

Which model of special educational needs?

The previous discussion has explored the limitations of the traditional, individual model of SEN. In this, the focus of attention is on the child or adult who has an impairment. We have argued that this approach has two major forms of limitation. First, it does not reflect a true functional analysis of the situation. To give a simple example, a child with a mild to moderate hearing loss may function very differently in two classrooms.

> Sarah has a 50dB hearing loss, with some fluctuations: her hearing is worse when she has one of her frequent colds/ear infections. Ms Smith knows of her hearing problems, having discussed her with the peripatetic teacher of the hearing impaired, whom she meets each month to check

progress. Ms Smith ensures that before any instruction is given to the class, she has Sarah's attention by gaining eye contact and giving an agreed signal before asking the class to listen. She always addresses the class near and facing Sarah, and checks that Sarah has understood afterwards. When teaching the class, Ms Smith operates the same system but prepares Sarah and checks her understanding by brief pre- and post-input sessions with her.

Now think of a classroom where the teacher 'treats Sarah like all the others', talks to the class as she walks around the room, engages Sarah in her turn for individual or small group work as any other child. In both settings Sarah has an impairment, but her degree of disablement is different. Both teachers may have the same attitude to Sarah, both believing they are treating her appropriately and valuing her equally. Yet the effects may be very different.

Hence, as this example indicates, an analysis of children's disabilities and needs must take account of both their own disabilities and impairment, but also the environment (e.g. classroom) in which they operate. That is, disability and needs are determined by an *interaction* between within child and external factors. Secondly, the pure individual model fails to recognise the wider disablement caused by society's failure to address the needs of people with disabilities and, in a political sense, diverts attention and action.

This issue is comparable to the discussion of integration and inclusion (Chapter 8) and comes down to alternative conceptualisations of SEN and disability. The social model has focused primarily on the impact of society *causing* disablement and may play down, even deny, the importance of the impairment itself. Take for example Oliver's criticism of conductive education:

> Lest anyone should be unclear about what's wrong with conductive education, its pursuit of nearly walking to the detriment of family, social and community life for many disabled children flies in the face of experiences of disability (*sic*) people throughout the world. The problems that disabled people face are the product of discrimination and oppression, not the consequences of different functioning abilities. (Oliver 1992, p.42)

But is this a reasonable position? Clearly, given our first analysis, this cannot be acceptable. Each disability has multiple causes, which may vary in their relative contributions. For example, remaining with hearing impairment, the primary factor affecting a newborn baby with a profound hearing loss is the impairment itself. However, as the child develops, the quality and quantity of support of various kinds will influence the child's development. As a deaf adult with positive conventional attainments (academic, social skills etc.) the major influence on employment and promotion may be social attitudes to deaf people.

Also, can we assume that people with impairments do not consider these negatively, as limiting factors in their lives, independent of any views they might have of social oppression? Is it ever correct to try to reduce, even overcome, an impairment? For example, if cochlea implants can be successful, we will reduce the deaf community, perhaps even, with this or another intervention, eradicate the community altogether. Is this genocide or liberation? And if medical advances do lead to fewer deaf children being born, will this situation necessarily lead to a lower valuing of those in a smaller deaf community?

The strength of the social model has been political: it has focused attention on societal failings and has given a direction to the actions of people with disabilities and others. These are important and necessary elements in a political process. Struggles of black people against racism and women against sexism, for example, may be seen as parallels. But the parallels are limited. Racism and sexism are both societal reactions to individuals and groups but, other than in rare cases, people do not change race or biological sex: race may be redefined socially, and gender roles may vary. However, with respect to disability, it is possible for individuals to 'improve' their position: a person with limited mobility may develop the ability to walk; a deaf child may be helped to hear; a child with severe reading difficulties may develop reading competence; the distressed and disturbing adolescent may change both self-image and behaviour. In each case such individuals may see these changes as positive.

Model of disability and values

Let us stand back for a moment. Do we imagine that in the past when children's difficulties were conceptualised as 'within child' that professionals paid *no* attention to external factors? Presumably this is not the case if such children were brought within the education system where, it was assumed, they could benefit. Hence, even if the causes of the difficulties were seen as lying within the child, the education system was seen as a means of affecting their future development. But this was not the case for all. It was only in 1970 that legislation was passed ending a system where some children were deemed 'ineducable'. Also, many children had relatively little contact with so-called 'normal' children. In the past 'ineducable' children may have been at home or in subnormality hospitals; others were in segregated special schools, some of which were residential.

Whatever the ideas held by professionals regarding causation and options for educational support to aid development, social attitudes, both within the professionals (and indeed the parents and children) but also within society at large, were important factors. These attitudes include those influenced by the legislation as the law and social attitudes interact. In other cases, society's attitudes lead legislation, as with the position in 1996 regarding availability of firearms following incidents such as the Dunblane School massacre. Legislation was put before Parliament following a national outcry and a sustained campaign by the parents of the children murdered, supported by the media.

The point of issue for us is this: what do these approaches, these definitions and conceptualisations indicate about the *values* we hold? If we consider the three models discussed first, what we shall now call the *individual model*, we can tease out possible values, but this must be done with care. Reflection on the individual model indicates that it is not *inherently* negative. Following the medical model of some diseases, diagnosis may lead to cure; or if cure is not possible, treatment which alleviates suffering. However, the problem is that it can be demonstrated that the causes of *all* children's difficulties in functioning are the result of an interaction of child with environmental factors. It is the *relative* influence of each factor which is important. Furthermore, although some actions do not necessarily follow, failure to attend to environmental issues has generated decisions leading to devaluing experiences. For example, the fact that a child has profound and multiple learning and physical difficulties does not necessarily lead to a decision that he or she should be removed from, or have limited access to the rest of society. However, such a child does not fit easily into a school system geared to children without such difficulties (e.g. Chapter 5). Thus, many of the negative and devaluing actions regarding children with difficulties have arisen by *default*.

These examples indicate the other side of legislation from that specifically intended to address children with SEN, and suggest that other government action has undervalued and even devalued these children. But who are children with special educational needs? We have so far used this term uncritically, yet its definition, and even the conceptualisation of 'special needs' and 'special educational needs' is controversial. In this next section we shall explore these issues.

Differentiation and values

The thrust of our argument so far has been that a workable model of special educational needs must take account both of 'within child' and 'within environment' factors, and their interaction, and the further interaction of all these three variables with time. We have provided a general model, but we would argue that this applies at the level of specific components of the system.

For example, let us return to Sarah learning in a classroom. Previously we focused on the teaching; the other major element to consider is the curriculum content. Should this be the same for all children? Should Sarah cover the identical programme of study as every other child – indeed, should all children cover exactly the same programme of study? In practice several responses can be observed. Take a typical non-selective school, whether primary or secondary, drawing from its local neighbourhood. At the start of the year the children will enter the class with a range of levels of ability – in reading, spelling, vocabulary, mathematics, general knowledge and so on. The teacher may present the same material to all. But this will result in some children being faced with work that is too difficult or too easy. In practice, therefore, work is differentiated. This may be by outcome whether of *quantity* (e.g. to expect a story of two pages from one child, half a page from another) or *quality* (all children produce two pages, but spellings, verbal expressions etc may vary). Alternatively, differentiation may be by task. For example, one child may be learning to calculate subtraction of hundreds, tens and units, while another is learning to count to ten.

The value issue that arises here is this: what do these styles of differentiation imply for the value which is placed on the child? And, secondly, are the values that may be found to be held by study of classrooms necessarily inevitable?

The position of the National Curriculum Council in its 1989 publication *A Curriculum for All* on children with SEN was clear: differentiation was seen as a positive approach to enhancing children's learning by adapting the total learning experience to the needs of the child.

However, not all educationists take such a positive line. For some, the setting of alternative objectives, or different patterns of teaching (e.g, withdrawal), or arranging different learning tasks, are considered inappropriate. Some claim that differentiation, therefore, is a negative process which, implicitly, devalues the child. This debate has been examined in detail by Norwich (1994) who suggests:

> This can be represented as the tension between a negative view of 'difference' as indicating lower status, less value and perpetuating inequalities and unfair treatment, versus a positive view which sees 'difference' as recognising what is relevant to an individual's learning and development needs. (p.293)

Our position is the same as that of Norwich. We recognise that differentiation may have negative aspects. The following are some examples. Secondary modern schools provided a differentiated education at that macro-structural level, but they also received less finance and reinforced a social and education division. Special classes in some schools were set up in the past to cater for pupils who were considered problems; they received a limited curriculum, reducing these pupils' later opportunities. Recently OFSTED have made criticism of classrooms where differentiation has been characterised by inappropriately low expectations (e.g. OFSTED 1996a). However, as Norwich argues, there is an inherent tension when making educational arguments between addressing values of equality and individuality. Neither can be addressed properly without considering the other, and the final arrangement must be a balance. Furthermore, Norwich argues that a second tension arises when a school or individual teacher decides a group's goals. For example, should the school aim to improve the average attainment of all pupils, or enhance the attainment of a subset such as the most able or those with SEN? This could result in: smaller classes for some (and hence larger for others); additional facilities (e.g. lunchtime sessions) for some; accelerated streams; 'special' classes (again). Norwich argues that:

the more you aim to raise the average attainment as the teaching goal, the greater is likely to be the variation in attainment; while the more the goal is to reduce variations in attainment levels, the lower average attainment will be. (p.300.)

This issue is picked up by Jesson (1996) and Fitzgibbon (1996) in their analyses of GCSE grades. Using a formula for measuring 'value added' (i.e. the improvement made differentially by the school given the abilities of pupils on entry) it is possible to plot schools as providing 'value added', or not, by comparing the performance of individual pupils at GCSE against that predicted by earlier performance (e.g. abilities of pupils on entry at 11 years). This has been welcomed and promoted by educationists and the Labour Party as a means of overcoming the criticism that raw data (i.e. numbers of GCSE grades A to C, for example) do not take account of widely different school intakes, and so flatter middle class (and independent) schools, while unfairly representing schools with socially disadvantaged intakes, where many pupils have English as a second language, or where there are large numbers of pupils with SEN.

Astute head teachers, by examining the location of their schools on the scattergram, may realise that their current performance ('not adding value') might be reversed if the proportion of pupils gaining 5 GCSE's at grades A–C went up by only a small amount, say 5 per cent, whereas this would not occur if the percentage of grades A–G went up by the same amount. Would such a head not be tempted to target positively the children who are most likely to ensure that outcome?

Differentiation, therefore, is a complex issue. Not only are the practical tasks of differentiating the curriculum and teaching difficult, both the rationale and consequences require careful consideration.

Values and SEN

In this chapter we have considered the relationships between disability and special educational needs with value systems. There is a clear tension between the positions taken by those who advocate the social model of disability and those who focus on the difficulties experienced by children which they consider to be related to inherent 'within child' impairments. We have also argued that differentiation in education, whether of aims, objectives, teaching methods, curriculum content, assessment, specific tasks, methods of monitoring or motivation, is not straightforward. While for some the focus is on enhancing learning, others wish to accentuate equality and a sense of belonging, which may be undermined by any differentiation in this list.

However, the line we prefer to advance is that there is no simple answer as these different perspectives all have degrees of validity. What is necessary, therefore, is to recognise several issues.

First, the development of all children is enhanced or impeded by an interaction between their own relative strengths and weaknesses and those of the environment and these vary over time. This model has been termed compensatory interaction and is presented in Figure 1.1.

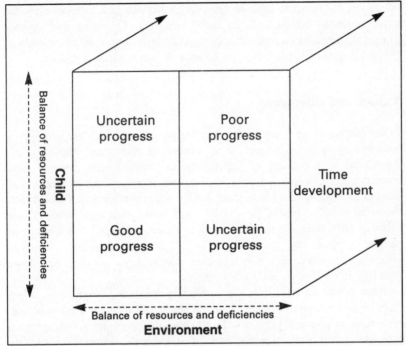

Figure 1.1 A model of compensatory interaction
Source: Wedell and Lindsay 1980

In this model, the negative influence of the environment might include inappropriate support for the child or even rejection, but also takes account of the child's own inherent problems (e.g. cerebral palsy) but does *not* imply a one-to-one relationship between 'having a disorder' and restricted potential. In addition to positive environmental resources, the child will also have personal strengths, though these combinations will vary from one child to another.

Secondly, we stress the need to separate the theoretical and ideological from the empirical. For example, it may be the case that certain conceptualisations of SEN appear likely to lead to negative outcomes, but do they? In Chapter 8 we address this issue in more detail: inclusive education may be supported on the basis of values of equality and belongingness, for example, but are the outcomes for the pupils themselves actually in accord with the aims of the exercise?

Thirdly, we consider it important to recognise that the values which lead to these different positions may not be easily reconcilable, and hence that practical solutions are inherently limited to partial or focused success. For example, the aim of ensuring that all children with SEN belong to their school and class may not be easily reconcilable with the aim of ensuring they all have the optimal opportunity to improve their academic attainments. This is not, as is often argued, simply a question of finance, but rather of optimal resources for the objectives specified. This is not to argue against inclusive education, but rather to urge the need for greater analysis. Consequently, the value positions which underlie such aims (e.g. belonging and optimal progress) should be recognised as being valid and worthwhile in themselves, but in a degree of tension. It is the balance of values which is crucial.

Values and dilemmas

In this chapter we have argued that deciding provision for children with special educational needs is subject to a number of dilemmas. These include consideration of equality of opportunity, as these children demand more resources. For example, a school which spends money to ensure access to all parts of its building could have spent that finance in another way. This indicates the relative value placed on children and adults (teachers, visitors) with mobility difficulties. On the other hand, as shown in Chapter 5, a school may decide to place 'the good of the others' first. Professionals, including educational psychologists, may also have dilemmas, as one of us has shown (Lindsay 1996; Lindsay and Colley 1995).

Some dilemmas arise from the conflicting demands of legislation, others from limited resources to meet identified needs, still others as a result of non-resolution of personal priorities. In all cases the processes which are gone through reflect the value systems of individuals, institutions and the legislation. In this book we shall examine a variety of such dilemmas as part of our attempt to explore the values explicitly and implicitly shaping the educational lives of children with special education needs.

Chapter 2

Values and Legislation

Geoff Lindsay

Legislation is based upon questions of value and also practical considerations. Sometimes these fit well together, but at others there are tensions. Further, on occasion a single piece of legislation may contain a variety of elements, deriving from different value positions, for example, the Education Reform Act 1988 (see Lawton 1988). In this chapter I shall review some of the major legislation, reports and white papers in order to identify the value position(s) taken by the Government in its legislative programme. I shall examine the implications of this programme for children with special educational needs.

The Warnock Report 1978

In a sense, the setting up of the Warnock Committee and the publication of its Report (Department of Education and Science 1978) make a significant statement about children with SEN. This was the first comprehensive examination of 'handicapped children and young people' as they were then termed. Of course, the corollary is that the fact that it had taken until the mid-1970s to have such a committee also spoke volumes about the place of 'the handicapped' in government priorities.

A key statement of principle and values is to be found, almost as a footnote, at the end of Chapter 1; General Approach:

> Those who work with children with special educational needs should regard themselves as having a crucial and developing role in a society which is now committed, not merely to tending and caring for its handicapped members, as a matter of charity, but to educating them, as a matter of right and to developing their potential to the full. (para. 1.11)

Children's rights

The Warnock Report stressed the need to accord all children with SEN the same rights as other children and to develop each child to the full. This value position is important as previously the approach had been to focus on sub-groups of children defined by their disability. Legislation had been directed at the education of, for example, the blind and the deaf (see Chapter 2 of the Warnock Report or Cole 1989 for useful summaries of the history). It may seem unbelievable now, but until the end of the 1960s 'mentally handicapped' children were deemed incapable of being educated in school. When the Education (Handicapped Children) Act 1970 was enacted in April 1971,

> 24,000 children in junior training centres and social care units, 8,000 in about 100 hospitals, and an uncertain number at home or in private institutions ceased to be treated as being mentally deficient and became entitled to special education. (DES 1978, para. 2.67)

Labelled severely educationally subnormal (ESN(S)), these children and young people at last had a right to education: a right that had been secured after a long struggle by many parents. This development also led to the creation of about 400 new special schools, many in old, unsuitable buildings. To meet this problem a major slice of the special school building programme (42 per cent in 1974–75; 33 per cent in 1975-76) was allocated to ESN(S) places, so reflecting the value now being placed on giving these children educational opportunities, albeit within a segregated system.

Parents as partners

A whole chapter in the report was devoted to parents as partners. Not only was this a matter of parental rights, it was of great practical importance. Also, the report stressed with regard to the relationship of parents and professionals: 'It is a partnership and ideally an equal one.' (para. 9.6)

In practice, the Report tended to dwell more on the support parents might require than their proactive contributions, but the value of parents as central to achieving the objectives for children with SEN was clear.

Continuum of disability and need

The Report stressed, on the basis of research findings as well as the experience of its members and advisers, that children do not fit neatly into disability types. Rather, each child is an individual, and has a range of needs consequent upon his or her unique set of strengths and weaknesses. Furthermore, these arise from both within child factors and the response from the environment: school and family in particular. Hence this conceptualisation stressed the value of individuality of each child.

Assessment and analysis

The Warnock Report is often remembered for its introduction of the idea of stages of assessment, later incorporated into the Code of Practice (DfE

1994). However, it is worth reminding ourselves that the Committee clearly set a high value on identification and assessment. This was not the simplistic process of IQ determining the appropriate type of school. On the contrary, assessment should be *effective*, and to be such, it was argued, needed to be carried out over time, to involve parents, to make use of a variety of methods, and to address both the child and the context:

> The educational psychologist, for example, needs time, not only to carry out tests, but also to observe the child in a variety of settings, taking into account factors such as curiosity, drive, attentiveness, distractibility and the influence of different types of surroundings. He needs to obtain the observations of teachers and others who know the child. (para. 4.30.)

Needs-led provision

Provision for children with SEN must be the result of the resolution of several tensions. With respect to the curriculum, the Report stresses that 'the general aims of education are the same for all children' (para. 11.2). However, to address the specific curricular needs of individual children at specific times, a differentiated curriculum is necessary.

Similarly, with respect to location, the Committee concluded that its analysis of continua of needs must result in a range of special educational provision. Most of the one in five children likely to require special educational provision at some time during their school career will be in mainstream, but the Committee stressed that they saw a continuing role for special schools. The Report was probably as detailed in its discussion of the role of special schools as of supporting children with SEN in mainstream schools. Section 10 of the Education Act 1976, the Committee argued, did not simply address *location* (it was widely seen as supporting the furtherance of integration) but also of *quality*. Taking these two factors into account leads to dilemmas which must be reconciled by careful planning.

The Report makes sound recommendations regarding planning, teacher training and resourcing to meet children's SEN, but with respect to integration and special schools there is a strong theme of caution. While this is appropriate, the tone comes across not as positive regarding developments in integration, with necessary support, but rather stresses building on the good practice of special schools.

Concluding comments

The Warnock Report was, and continues to be, a very important and highly influential report. Although it is often seen only as the basis for the mechanisms and paraphernalia of later legislation (e.g. the statement, stages of assessment) the Report set down key value positions, albeit not specified as such, which guided their proposals. These cannot be linked easily to support for inclusive education, for example. Rather, they reflect a more fundamental value position with regard to children with SEN, together with value positions on which a system should be built.

The Education Act 1981

The importance of the Warnock Report is evident from examination of the Education Act 1981. Key concepts from the report are embedded in the Act, which consequently reflects the Report's value system. As with the Report, the fact that there should be a comprehensive law for SEN both reflects well on government, recognising the importance of the issues, and badly on earlier administrations.

The value placed on individual needs being recognised and analysed by high quality assessment in partnerships with parents, for example, is directly related to the Warnock Report. However, the Act also stressed, as indeed the Report had discussed, the need to recognise practicalities, particularly with regard to finance. Hence, while the basic position was that provision should be made within a mainstream school, this was subject to its being an efficient use of resources, and not interfering adversely with the education of other children. Integration was supported – up to a point.

In practice, the Act was not accompanied by any new money to support its implementation. It is interesting to contrast this with the Education Act 1996, currently going through Parliament, which specifies where new money is needed. For example, 'development of Baseline Assessment' is to be funded at £300000 for 1997–8 and £700000 per year thereafter for development costs met by central Government – although the £1 million estimated to be needed to run the programme appears to be coming out of local government funds.

Thus, the Government supported the values of addressing the needs of children with SEN, and the basic value positions taken by the Warnock Committee, but did not see this as an area of such priority that it should divert resources, although in the event local government did so anyway.

The Children Act 1989

The Children Act 1989 brought together legislation 'fragmented across the face of the statute book' (Department of Health 1989, p.1). It was the result of much consultation with child welfare and legal interests before the Bill, and subject to long debate in Parliament, unfortunately guillotined owing to other matters in the Commons. Although it was the first Bill to be introduced into the House of Lords in the 1988–9 session, it was the last to receive Royal Assent. According to White, Carr and Lowe 1990 (p.vii.) its passing was a 'damn close run thing'.

Central to the Act is the core value of the welfare of the child. As stated in the opening clause:

Welfare of the child
1. (1) When a court determines any question with respect to –
   (a) the upbringing of a child; or
   (b) the administration of a child's property or the application of any income arising from it,
   the child's welfare shall be the court's paramount consideration.

Consequently, as the Department of Health's guidance states:

... whilst the courts are to take into account all the relevant surrounding circumstances, including, for example, the wishes of the parents, at the end of the day they must do what is best for the child' (para. 1.20).

In addition, as stated in Section 1 (3) (a) of the Act, a court shall have regard to:

(a) the ascertainable wishes and feelings of the child concerned (considered in the light of his age and understanding).

In her commentary, Judith Masson (1990) stresses that the emphasis shall be on the objective assessment of the needs of the individual child.

If we examine the Act for its value system, we find the following:

Welfare of the child paramount

It is clear that the Act requires the interests of the child to be placed first and foremost, above the wishes of parents and others.

Parental responsibility and the importance of the family

However, the Act reinforces and extends the importance of the family through its emphasis on parental responsibility. This extends even when the child is being looked after by the Local Authority.

Practical, not legalistic, remedies

By focusing on child welfare, the Act stresses the need to be practical. For example, it is stressed that a child's interest may be damaged by delays. In addition, the dilemmas that arise from tensions reconciling needs are recognised. It is necessary, for example, to strike a balance between protection from harm that can arise from abuse, or failures in the family system, as opposed to harm that can be caused if children are subjected to unwarranted intervention in their family lives. In this context, there is stress in the Department of Health's guidelines on Protection from 'Protection'.

The Education Act 1993

In most respects, the 1993 Education Act was a reiteration of its 1981 predecessor. There were slight, but important changes of wording, but the essential set of principles remained similar. However, the changes are important.

The implementation of the 1981 Act was reviewed in two major ways; by government and by research. The House of Commons Education, Science and Arts Committee (1987) took evidence from a wide range of commentators, including voluntary bodies and professionals. The Audit Commission and Her Majesty's Inspectors were commissioned to examine the implementation of the Act. (Audit Commission/HMI 1992.)

The findings of these reports raised concerns. While the SEN profile had been raised, and there were many examples of good practice, the national practice was variable. For example, the Audit Commission and HMI found percentages of children with statements varied by a factor of four among 12 LEAs examined. There was, however, no correlation of the rate with a measure of disadvantage. Time taken to complete assessments was greater, on average, than the six months recommended targets among all 12 LEAs studied, and the worst had an average of nearly *three years*. The number of statements issued had increased nationally from 1987-91. Meanwhile the number of complaints to the Ombudsman and appeals to the Secretary of State had risen, the latter more than doubling between 1984 and 1991.

The report of the Audit Commission/HMI (1992) identified that the power of parents of children with SEN was limited. Their ability to appeal (see below, SEN Tribunal), their choice, and the accountability of LEAs to them were all constrained. The report's analysis makes gloomy reading. Refusals to assess, slowness in producing statements, and disagreement with the contents of statements were all identified as issues. Responsibilities of schools and LEAs were unclear, as were criteria for determining which child should be assessed, and which should be subject to a statement. Parents had fewer rights with regard to choice of provision. In terms of the government's rhetoric it may be concluded that there was certainly diversity, but choice was limited.

These reports provided a major criticism of the operation of the Act. The act was inconsistent, inefficient and clearly did not meet the objective of ensuring each child with SEN received a quality assessment, and provision to meet the needs identified. The response of the Government was to add to the new Act two important powers: to provide guidance on identification and assessment, and to set up SEN Tribunals.

Code of Practice

The inconsistency with respect to identification and assessment practices was addressed by the Code of Practice (DfE, 1994). This is a non-statutory document, being guidance, but all to whom the Code applies 'have a statutory duty to have regard to it; they must not ignore it' (Foreword, para. 6). The Code of Practice is essentially concerned with the provision of practical guidance to LEAs schools and professionals, focusing on the mechanics of identification and assessment, the five stages of assessment, statements and annual reviews; it is not directly concerned with provision *per se*. However, the Code does signify five 'fundamental principles,' namely:

- The needs of all pupils who may have special educational needs throughout, or at any time during, their school careers must be addressed; the Code recognises that there is a continuum of needs and a continuum of provision which may be made in a wide variety of different forms.
- Children with special educational needs require the greatest possible access to broad and balanced education, including the National Curriculum.
- The needs of most pupils will be met in the mainstream, and without a statutory assessment or statement of special educational needs. Children with special educational needs, including children with statements of special educational needs, should, where appropriate and taking into account the wishes of their parents, be educated alongside their peers in mainstream schools.
- Even before he or she reaches compulsory school age a child may have special educational needs requiring the intervention of the LEA as well as the health services.
- The knowledge, views and experience of parents are vital. Effective assessment and provision will be secured where there is the greatest possible degree of partnership between parents and their children and schools, LEAs and other agencies.

These principles are to be welcomed. They assert the importance of assessing needs early, of entitlement to a broad and balanced curriculum, and inclusive education.

The Code has been embraced and found useful in a way that so many Government outpourings are not. The detailed guidance provided is clear and thoughtful, generally reflecting sound practice already existing, or that which follows from the above principles. Criteria for deciding to make a statutory assessment were included to meet criticism that practice was variable in the absence of such guidance. These have been found useful, up to a point – there are still many questions left unanswered, and the numbers of children with statements have continued to increase.

Special Educational Needs Coordinators

Paragraph 2.14 of the Code of Practice specified a new professional: the special educational needs co-ordinator (SENCO) with a formidable list of responsibilities. From being a marginal person in many schools, the teacher with responsibility for SEN soon became a central and key member of the management system. In this respect, an important benefit of the Code has been to bring special needs to the top of agendas in schools when budgets, staffing, curriculum and the full range of management issues are discussed.

The demands on these new professionals (about 26,000) are formidable and training has been limited as Lewis *et al.* (1997) have shown. While some were previously SEN specialists, albeit mainly as teachers rather than coordinators, managers and policy developers, others were elevated almost overnight. Many educational psychologists would have had my experience of a school nominating a teacher (or in this case two with a job share) with no previous expertise, who then asked me for support. This is not, of course, a criticism of the school but reflects both the positive response to the need for a SENCO, and the lack of government finance to allow proper training. The workloads can be formidable and the range of expertise expected daunting (Lewis *et al.* 1997). What is remarkable, and encouraging, is the extent to which so many SENCOs have tackled this job with professionalism.

The SEN Tribunal

The report of the Audit Commission/HMI (1992) indicated that there was a problem with respect to appeals by parents where the LEA refused to assess, or refused to issue a statement, or where the parent did not agree with the content of a statement. Local appeals were rare and the number of appeals to the Secretary of State was low, but increasing. Two thirds of appeals to the Secretary of State were found in favour of LEAs, and the time taken was between 9 and 12 months on average, despite the DfE target of 6 months. Finally, complaints of maladministration to the Ombudsman were also increasing, from under 10 in 1987–8 to over 25 by 1990–91. The report was also critical of the content of statements, including their vagueness, but was sympathetic to the dilemmas faced by LEAs: 'The LEA is under financial pressure: it has an open-ended obligation to an ill-defined group.' (para. 47.)

The SEN Tribunal was set up by the Education Act 1993, clauses 177–181. Work started in 1994, and by the time of its second annual report some patterns were emerging (SEN Tribunal 1996). By the end of the year appeals were coming in at about 35 *per week*, considerably above the original estimate. More staff were taken on and the target average time of four and a half months for dealing with appeals was met once more. The majority of parents were not represented, but 11 per cent had lawyers and 15 per cent had other representatives. The President of the Tribunal asserted his wish that the proceedings should be as informal as possible. Although it is the parent who brings the appeal on behalf of the child, the Education (Special Educational Needs) Bill presented by Lord Campbell of Alloway in 1996 sought to allow that a child 'if of sufficient understanding' should also be empowered to bring an appeal.

The statistics in the report indicate that the majority of appeals were against the content of the statement (37%) followed by failure to assess (24%). The SEN area most frequently represented was literacy (including specific learning difficulties) at 39.6%, over three times as prevalent as the next most frequent, moderate learning difficulties (11.1%), apart from 'other' (14.4%). Overall, the balance of judgements was to uphold the appeal, although this average hides a difference between appeals against Parts 2 and 3 of the statement (the specification of needs and provision to meet needs) where 244 were upheld and 50 dismissed, compared with appeals against Part 4 (the specification of the school) where the balance was 181 to 210.

The SEN Tribunal, therefore, may be seen as a positive development in the sense that parents have a quicker route to appeal, and have a good chance of having their appeal upheld. On the other hand, the high number of appeals suggests difficulties with implementing the legislation.

Education Reform Act 1988

The previous discussion has focused on legislation specifically concerned with the rights of individual children. However, while this programme was underway, there was a more pervasive programme being developed. This was concerned with the education system as a whole and, together with other legislation aimed at reducing the powers of local authorities, was designed to change fundamentally this power balance between local and national government, school and the parents.

The Education Act 1988 (ERA) was a comprehensive legislative attack on the education system, designed to change radically its operation. The introduction of the National Curriculum, Local Management of Schools (LMS) and new types of schools such as Grant Maintained (GM) schools, arose from a sense of unease generated at a high visibility political level by Jim Callaghan's Ruskin College speech in 1978. The legislation, as Lawton (1988) has shown is derived from contradicting philosophical and value positions. Local Management of Schools and GM Schools represent attempts to introduce free market, 'hands off' approaches. The National Curriculum, its attendant assessment programme, and the development of the Office for Standards in Education (OFSTED) with its four year cycle of school inspections, represent attempts by the state to ensure standards.

The impact on children with SEN appears not to have been considered by developers of the ERA. Despite their contradictions, the thrust of *both* ideological strands, in practice, has been difficult to implement with regard to SEN. For example, LMS was not workable for special schools, and a supplementary scheme was required; the appropriate reconciliation in curriculum terms between the requirements for all children to follow the National Curriculum, their entitlement to a broad and balanced curriculum (and not some second-rate, watered down version), and the appropriate detail of such a curriculum for individuals is still being worked out.

Choice and Diversity

In 1992 the Government produced a statement of intent, a 'new framework for schools' entitled *Choice and Diversity* (Department for Education 1992). In the forward, John Major, the Prime Minister stated:

> The Government are determined that every child in this country should have the very best start in life. The drive for higher standards in schools has been a hallmark of the Government over the last decade. Now this White Paper carries this great programme of reform further forward. (Foreword, p.iii)

Encouraging words, but how was this brave new world to ensure higher standards for children with SEN? Chapter 9 was devoted to SEN. A commitment to the general principle of the 1981 Act was asserted including 'the emphasis on the needs of the individual child' and 'the rights of parents to be involved as partners' (para. 9.1). The concerns with the operation of the Act were to be addressed, including improved access to assessment and statements, and the right of parents to state a preference for their child's school, and an improved appeals procedure, through a tribunal. Commitment to integration was asserted, although the usual caveat regarding wise use of resources and provision of efficient education for the child's peers remained.

Hence, with respect to SEN specifically the White Paper did address major issues, in principle. What was not clear was how the principle of encouraging diversity and choice would be reconciled, for children with SEN, with the recognised need to plan provision for a specific minority of pupils.

Further evidence of the Government's concern for SEN appears in its consultation paper *Special Educational Needs: Access to the System* (Department for Education 1992b). This presented the problems of the implementation of the Education Act 1981 and made positive proposals. This consultation document provided a more detailed case than *Choice and Diversity*. Tribunals and improved procedures for assessment, for example, were addressed. Choice of school was another element, although in reality, the proposal was to give the right to express a preference, and for the LEA to take this *preference* into account.

While this document appropriately and positively addressed the concerns, the sting was in the tail. Paragraph 37 stated that the funding of SEN Tribunals would be met by diverting cash from the local authorities' revenue support grant and that 'the other measures proposed should be cost neutral for authorities'. In other words, LEAs would receive *less* money despite expecting them to assess children more quickly, more professionally and, by implication, in greater numbers, let alone support parents and children in making *informed* 'choice' of school.

Conclusion

In this chapter I have highlighted some of the major legislation which has a direct impact on children with SEN. Tracing development through from the mid-1970s, when the Warnock Committee was set up, to the mid-1990s, when an SEN Tribunal is up and running, it may be concluded that there is a clear sense of commitment to children with SEN. This is not simply a welfare–caring approach, but rather one that has gradually extended their legal rights.

These developments may be interpreted as a positive statement about successive governments' attitudes to children with SEN, although these changes did not come easily. They represent the outcomes of long and hard campaigns by voluntary bodies, professionals and individual parents on behalf of their children (e.g. Peter 1995).

We may welcome and celebrate these changes, but then quickly recognise that for every two steps forward there has been at least one step back, for while this legislation was coming onto the statute books, other laws were producing major dilemmas.

The challenges come from two sources. Firstly, the financial situation of the country, and individual LEAs and schools, has resulted in a limitation on developments. There has not been a significant input into the system to enable changes in legislation to be put into operation. For example, the necessary changes to physical access have been a fraction of those necessary to enable all schools to welcome children with particular physical disabilities. Coopers and Lybrand (1993) report that children with physical disabilities have access to all teaching space in only 26% of primary and 10% of secondary schools. Access to even three quarters of teaching space is available in only 46% of primary schools. Acoustic conditions are often not satisfactory to provide a reasonable environment for children with hearing impairment. Furthermore, training has not been developed, and indeed has commonly been cut, along with support staff. At the same time, class size has increased. These financial realities reflect priorities, and hence value positions.

Secondly, other legislation, or other sections of the same legislation (e.g., the Education Act 1993) has set up direct conflicts. For example, there is a recognition that provision for SEN must be planned if it is to be effective, comprehensive and efficient, yet a cornerstone of Government thinking has been a market forces approach, which promotes *diversity*. In some cases diversity is real, there are now more types of school, for example, but in others it is illusory. There is a fear at this time (early 1997) that Government legislation on nursery vouchers has reduced the numbers of pre-school playgroups; LEAs have needed to close schools to remove 'excess places' from the system. Consequently, the other cornerstone, choice, has been reduced in many cases. Add to this the fact that increasingly some schools are choosing pupils, rather than parents and children choosing schools.

LEAs, therefore, are faced with a need to reduce spending overall, to delegate increasing amounts to schools and to close schools to remove excess places. At the same time, they are expected to make provision for children's special educational needs (whether direct or by requiring the school to do so), to plan SEN provision and to act as a support for children with SEN and their parents. Schools are in a similar position, being forced by league tables to seek higher and higher examination success and reduced absenteeism, while surviving OFSTED inspections. All of this is taking place in a public ethos, promoted by Her Majesty's Chief Inspector of Schools (HMCI), where blame and selective, questionable and clearly invalid reading of statistics are used in the belief that they will promote improved performance.

The results of the interaction of these different laws, the particular ideology of the Government, and the public representation of Senior civil servants, such as HMCI, may be seen as in contradiction to the positive and progressive elements of the SEN legislation itself. There will always be a tension between lack of resources and aspirations, and between the need to distribute resources to those who need extra to achieve equality of opportunity and those for whom extra resources will have a markedly enhanced effect on producing excellence. But the period of the Conservative administration was marked by a significant shift away from resourcing the disadvantaged to a world where personal responsibility, and individual rather than collective action have been considered preferable.

As Cordingly and Kogan (1993) argue persuasively, this legislation has rejected a system which has social cohesion as a core value. Their analysis of the values exemplified by legislation and the *Choice and Diversity* White Paper suggests also that efficiency cannot be regarded as a core value either.

Whether or not the injunction by Norman Tebbit, a former chairman of the Conservative Party, to the unemployed to 'get on your bike' is helpful, to children with SEN this is inappropriate even as a metaphor. Individual responsibility is one thing, but our young people need support in order to achieve independence, a status some may never achieve. Thus, the political agenda for the next decade must be to re-examine the current legislation beyond the specific legal rights of children with SEN, to the realisation of meeting needs based on those rights. This will require a re-examination of the value system on which a legislative programme is to be built.

Chapter 3

Ethnic Minority Communities and Values in Special Education

Martin Desforges

Concepts of Special Education are intimately bound up with aims and purposes of mainstream education, and before looking at specific issues around special education we need to consider the values reflected by mainstream education, and how they are perceived by the various ethnic minority communities. The variety of terms used in this area can be a source of disagreement and confusion, interpreted in different ways by different groups. For example, Grant and Brookes (1996) comment on the pejorative connotations of 'multicultural', 'ethnic minority' and 'bilingual'. Katz (1996) explores the post-modernist critiques of theories of race, racism and anti-racism.

In this chapter the terms 'black' and 'ethnic minority' will be used. In most cases a specific group will be named when referring to an ethnic minority group. Black is used in the political sense, to include all those groups experiencing racism within British society because of the ethnic group to which they belong. It includes African, African–Caribbean, Asian and Chinese groups.

An interactionist perspective of special educational needs (SEN) is taken in this chapter. Whether a child will be seen by educational professionals as having special educational needs will be influenced by strengths and weaknesses of the child as well as by the educational stress and support factors in operation for that individual – class size, strengths and weaknesses of the class teacher and the school, criteria against which the school is judged to be succeeding, parental and community views of mainstream and special education. Other important factors will be the attitudes, beliefs and values of the main participants in the system towards SEN – parents, governors, politicians and educational professionals. Each of these groups contributes to the social construction of special educational needs.

Troyna and Carrington (1990) describe the monocultural educational ideologies of the 1960s and 1970s in which the message was 'forget the culture of your parents, discard any affiliation to your ethnic group. Being British is instead of, not as well as, being an ethnic group member'. (p.2)

If black pupils were doing less well than their white peers in exams, and this was clearly the case then for African–Caribbean pupils, the explanation was seen in terms of deficiencies in African–Caribbean culture, families and values.

Some went further, and claimed that a genetically determined difference in IQ between ethnic groups was the reason for poorer educational outcomes. Such a view is still held by members of the academic community (e.g. Herrnstein and Murray 1994). The Rampton Report (Department for Education and Science, 1981) with the give-away title of *'West Indian Children in OUR schools'* (my emphasis) subscribed to several pathological interpretations of African–Caribbean culture which lead to educational underachievement – poor family background, lack of parental support and inadequate socialisation. In the final report *'All Our Future'* (Department for Education and Science 1985) the very concept of institutionalised racism was dismissed as *'a confused and confusing concept'*. The establishment view was clear – the attitudes, beliefs and values of mainstream British culture, and their manifestation within the education system were not in any way responsible for the educational difficulties experienced by black pupils.

The argument presented here is that the mainstream education system has failed to meet the educational needs of many pupils from ethnic minority groups. They have performed less well in examinations, have been excluded more frequently, and more often inappropriately referred to segregated special schools. Ethnic minority parents have become suspicious of the values of the white education professionals involved in these processes, and rather than seeing special education as a way of getting specialist help, it is seen as helping mainstream education avoid making the necessary changes to meet the particular needs of pupils from the various ethnic minority groups. Evidence will be presented to support this argument, and to consider the exceptions to these main themes.

Education Reform Act

Prior to the 1988 Education Reform Act (ERA), in the absence of an explicit national education policy on race related matters, the campaign for promotion of antiracist education had come from the local level, helped by the 1976 Race Relations Act. Local Education Authorities (LEAs) had the duty and authority to encourage schools and Further Education colleges to take up educational policies formulated locally. The ERA has had two effects. It has allowed central government to take up powers in the areas of curriculum, assessment and pedagogy, and at the same time created a more fragmented and diverse school system with many more powers delegated to governing bodies, and a much reduced role for LEAs. Governing bodies now have increased powers in areas such as appointment of staff, exclusion of pupils, and responsibilities for the spending of the delegated school budget. The ERA has little to say on black pupils, and stresses a Christian, ethnocentric view of the education process. In the ten years since the 1988 Education Act, issues concerning equal opportunities for black pupils have been removed from the policy agenda (see Gillborn and Gipps 1996).

The National Curriculum, imposed on all state schools, but not on private ones, is characterised by a rejection of cultural pluralism, and a determined effort on the part of politicians and the quangos set up to implement the National Curriculum (National Curriculum Council, Schools Examination and Assessment Council, and now Schools Curriculum and Assessment Authority) to ensure that it reflects what they see as the values of white, British society. Unsuccessful attempts were made to include representatives with 'knowledge and experience of ethnic minorities' on these bodies (Tomlinson 1989). The National Curriculum is very much a nationalist curriculum, concerned not just with white supremacy, but with British, if not English supremacy. The chauvinism directed against the European Community is one manifestation of the political milieu in which this policy developed. The predominant religion is Christian, with little time devoted to study of the other main world religions. Literature is very much seen as that produced by English authors, rather than literature written in the English language. History is largely English history, with little chance to look at alternative perspectives on colonisation, empire and its impact on the cultural and economic lives of the recipients of this process. Modern languages are defined as modern European languages, ensuring that the common community languages of ethnic minority groups living in Britain are not part of the National Curriculum. The few LEAs which have made determined efforts to seek the views of black communities, and develop service delivery towards antiracist ends have been subject to ridicule from the media, and criticism from central government.

Tomlinson (1989) considers in detail the absence of race, ethnicity or even multicultural education from the 1988 Education Reform Act. This was not by accident, as the number of amendments to the Bill which were defeated or withdrawn give some indication of the government's position that there would be no explicit mention of race or related issues. One proposed amendment to the first clause of the Act, which requires the National Curriculum to prepare pupils 'for the opportunities, responsibilities and experiences of adult life' to add 'in a multicultural, multiracial society' was withdrawn. A proposal to include that all pupils should be educated to acquire positive attitudes to all ethnic groups was defeated.

It is against this background that Troyna and Carrington (1990) develop the thesis that the identity of black pupils is denied daily within the classroom. They suggest three ways that this disables the learning process of black pupils. Firstly, there are low self-expectations about the likely performance of black pupils in a white controlled education system. Secondly, they experience low motivation because of a feeling that the cards are stacked against their succeeding, and thirdly, low teacher expectations lead to a less than stimulating educational experience. There is much evidence that the education system has a long way to go before equality of opportunity becomes a reality for ethnic minority groups.

Educational attainments

There has been a considerable amount of research on educational outcomes for ethnic minority pupils in recent years (see Gillborn and Gipps 1996). On average, in the early years of infant and junior school, African–Caribbean pupils appear to achieve less well than white pupils, although recent results from baseline assessment instruments for five year olds in a number of authorities have provided evidence that African–Caribbean pupils enter schools with skill levels the same as those of white pupils (Desforges and Lindsay 1995). This clearly suggests that schools are failing to meet the needs of these pupils if they enter school with similar skill levels, but fail to make the same amount of progress in the early years.

A consistent finding has been the lower average attainments of Pakistani and Bangladeshi pupils in the early stages of education. This reflects the significance of fluency in English, and the relatively poor provision made to ensure cognitive development and the acquisition of basic literacy skills while acquiring English as a second language for this bilingual population (Desforges and Lindsay 1995).

At GCSE level, results indicate that regardless of ethnic origin, pupils from economically advantaged backgrounds achieve the highest levels, with girls performing better than boys from the same social class background. Clearly, any analysis of examination performance and ethnicity must take account of these factors (see Gillborn and Gipps 1996). Despite the difficulties in making these complex analyses, recent work on school effectiveness, using multi-level modelling, attempts to take account of factors such as class, gender, ethnic origin, socio-economic circumstances and school, in reaching conclusions about the relative importance of each of these factors in influencing educational outcomes. When results are analysed using these methods, African–Caribbean pupils are seen to do less well at GCSE than other groups, with the performance of African–Caribbean boys of particular concern. Indian pupils on average achieve more highly than other pupils from south Asia, and in some areas do better than white pupils. Pakistani pupils achieve less well than white pupils in many areas, with Bangladeshis performing less well than other groups.

It is difficult to tease out the various factors that may be leading to these results, but the marked improvement in exam performance of Bangladeshi pupils in certain LEAs (Tower Hamlets being the outstanding one), indicates the importance of school processes. Gillborn and Gipps (1996) summarise some of the emerging trends. White pupils tend to make better progress than ethnic minority pupils in primary school, whereas in secondary school Asian pupils make better progress than white pupils of the same social class. African–Caribbean pupils tend to do worst at both primary and secondary levels. Despite the better progress of some ethnic minority groups at secondary level, white pupils tend to leave school at 16+ with higher average attainments than other ethnic groups, a conclusion that is often overlooked.

Black pupils and special schools

In 1971 Bernard Coard published his book titled '*How the West Indian Child is made Educationally Subnormal in the British School System*'. He was reacting to the over-representation of black pupils in the Inner London Education Authority (ILEA) schools for children described then as being 'Educationally Subnormal (moderate) or ESN(M)'. Using ILEA statistics for 1967 he found:

> in ILEA ESN(M) day schools over 28 per cent of all pupils were immigrant, compared with only 15 per cent immigrants in ordinary schools of ILEA. This situation is particularly bad for the West Indian, because three-quarters of all the immigrant children in these Educationally Sub-normal schools are West Indian, whereas West Indians are only half of the immigrant population in ordinary schools. (p.5)

The 1970 figures showed the trend continuing, with 34 per cent of the ESN(M) school population from immigrant communities, and 80 per cent of these immigrants in ESN(M) schools were West Indian. The same ILEA report gave figures for immigrant pupils whom head teachers thought had been wrongly placed in their schools (see Table 3.1). Thirteen of the nineteen schools surveyed had some misplaced pupils.

Table 3.1 Percentage of immigrant pupils misplaced (19 schools asked)

% misplaced	Number of schools
0–9%	3
10–19%	3
20–29%	3
30–39%	1
40–49%	2
70–79%	1

The survey also indicated that head teachers thought that immigrant pupils were four times more likely than white pupils to be wrongly placed. Even worse, despite the views of the head teachers, the numbers of immigrant pupils returning to mainstream schools from ESN(M) schools was low, around 7 per cent. The response of the ILEA to these findings was remarkable: 'Special schools for ESN children must continue to provide for immigrant children, even those with relatively high IQs, until more suitable alternatives can be found.' (p.11)

All this information and the publicity it received led to changes in practice, and the proportion of African-Caribbean pupils in schools for moderate learning difficulties declined throughout the 1970s. More recent work (Cooper *et al.* 1991) examined ethnic minority and gender distribution of staff and pupils in facilities for pupils with emotional and behavioural disorders in England and Wales. They sampled 355 schools and units for pupils described as having emotional and behavioural problems, and found that black boys and girls were over-represented in this type of special provision. Tomlinson (1994) wrote that it is difficult to sustain a medical or psychological model to understand and explain this situation. She interprets it as teacher and school participation in the social construction of deviant behaviour caused by the beliefs and perceptions of different racial and ethnic groups held by the white majority.

Recent studies of the assessment methods used by educational psychologists indicate the continued widespread use of standardised, norm-referenced instruments that may well be biased when used with ethnic minority groups (Desforges 1995; Desforges *et al*. 1995), suggesting yet another factor in the inappropriate placement of pupils from ethnic minority groups.

Exclusions

As well as issues of incorrect placement in special educational provision, concerns over exclusions have led many to question the value systems, sensitivity and knowledge base of LEAs and schools. Over the last ten years there has been an increasing awareness on the part of the African–Caribbean community of the much higher probability of African–Caribbean boys being excluded from schools. Both regional and national studies indicate that pupils from minority ethnic groups are excluded disproportionately. For example between 1974 and 1980 black pupils were four times more likely to be excluded from Birmingham schools than were white pupils. In Nottingham in 1991 black pupils were five times as likely to be excluded. *The Voice* (18 June 1991) reported that 85–90 per cent of pupils excluded from schools in six metropolitan authorities were black and male. Even more serious is the finding reported by the National Children's Bureau (1995) that in some cases the ethnicity of the pupil is directly related to the decision to exclude e.g. religious or cultural non-conformity, the failure to recognise cultural elements in incidents which occur within school, or the misdiagnosis and disregard for medical or educational problems specific to a particular ethnic group.

Gillborn and Gipps (1996) show that African–Caribbean pupils are six times more likely to be excluded from secondary schools than white pupils, and black African pupils three times more likely to be excluded. This study concludes that the over-representation of black pupils in exclusions is too large and too consistent over time and across regions to be a statistical artefact. Figures for permanent exclusions from all schools in England and Wales for the school year 1994–5 confirm this trend (Department for Education and Employment 1996) and are summarised in Table 3.2. African–Caribbean, black African and black other groups are between two and seven times as likely to be excluded from school than other groups, with Indian and Chinese pupils the least likely to be excluded.

A report from the Office of Her Majesty's Chief Inspector of Schools (1996a) of 16 LEAs reveals that only six provide data in a way that allows analysis of whether pupils from ethnic minority groups are differentially excluded, although in all six of these LEAs ethnic minority pupils were between two and six times more likely to be excluded than white. Recent OFSTED reports found evidence of good ethnic monitoring in less than one school in every two hundred, and that where schools have adopted a 'colour blind' approach, inequalities have continued.

Table 3.2 Permanent exclusions 1994–5 by ethnicity

Ethnic group	% of excluded pupils	% of school population
White	83.8	89.8
African–Caribbean	7.3	1.1
Black African	1.4	0.6
Black Other	1.7	0.8
Indian	0.9	2.7
Pakistani	2.0	2.1
Bangladeshi	0.4	0.8
Chinese	0.1	0.4
Other Ethnic Groups	2.3	1.5

Racism in education

There is considerable disagreement about the frequency and nature of racist behaviour in schools, with a number of quantitative studies (e.g. Tomlinson 1989) concluding that it is not a major issue. Troyna (1993) sees this as a result of inappropriate research methodologies, arguing for more qualitative research studies to help understand and combat racism in education. The methodologies used, including interviews and observations, provide important information on how systems work, but it is often difficult to generalise from the conclusions of particular studies.

Despite these reservations, such studies, together with information from other sources (Commission for Racial Equality 1988; National Children's Bureau 1990) provide evidence that racial harassment is not a rare event in educational institutions, and that it is not always recognised by teachers and other professionals in the system. It appears that Asian pupils are more likely to be victimised by white peers, but there are much higher levels of conflict between white teachers and African–Caribbean pupils at primary and secondary schools (see Gillborn and Gipps 1996). There are several studies analysing the processes where, despite the best intentions, teachers' actions can create and amplify conflict with African–Caribbean pupils (Wright 1986).

Stereotypical views held by white professionals of particular ethnic groups can be particularly damaging, but there are now several studies which challenge the validity of such perspectives. Bhogal (1995) notes the consistent finding that ethnic minority parents place a high positive value on education for their children. Where there are planned opportunities for parents to be involved with the school, parents will engage in serious and positive ways with teachers (see Tomlinson 1980). Atkinson (1992) challenges the view that arranged marriages lead to parents preventing Asian girls remaining in education and pursuing professional training. In an interview study with Year 10 Asian girls and their parents, she found little dissonance between the views of Asian parents and their daughters in their positive attitudes to post-16 education and aspirations to pursue professional careers.

Ng (1992) interviewed Chinese parents to discuss their views of special educational needs. She found that parents expected teachers to possess the expertise and responsibility to educate their children appropriately, and were unwilling to challenge the schools' authority. The cultural norm to respect authority and to be polite were seen by white professionals as passivity, even though parents were willing to cooperate in whatever ways teachers suggested.

All these studies make the same point. Rather than relying on the often ill-informed views of white professionals, there is a need to become aware of, and sensitive to, the range of cultural attitudes and values as they impinge on education, by direct discussion with parents. Such discussions are dependent on trust, and it is important to note that many of the workers cited above were themselves members of ethnic minority groups. There is a need for research on how better understanding between parents and professionals can be built up and to consider ways of recruiting more black professionals into the education system.

Grant and Brookes (1996) provide a response from the black community to the issue of stereotyping black pupils. Their starting point is that black pupils are often seen as problems. Multiculturalism with assimilation, integration and pluralist perspectives are seen as ways of accommodating black pupils within the education system with the aim to 'somehow dilute their detrimental effects on schools, but without resolving inherent conflicts'.

The perspective they develop is one of antiracism, with the aim of changing the nature of school to ensure it meets the needs of all pupils, and which creates an ethos where racism in all its manifestations within the school community is addressed (see Catholic Working Party on Multiracial Education 1984).

Grant and Brookes note that the terms used to describe black people – race, ethnicity, immigrant – all have popular definitions with pejorative social and political connotations. These terms all serve to keep black pupils as an underclass, reinforcing the stereotype of the misbehaving, underachieving black pupil. In academic psychology the debate on black–white differentials in education (e.g. Herrnstein and Murray 1994), and the effects of bilingualism on cognitive development (see Romaine 1994) have had a fundamental influence on teacher training and the education system. All these have created a climate where black behaviour is seen as problem behaviour. Writing in the *Times Educational Supplement*, Klein (6 September 1996 p.13.) refers to studies over the last twenty years that have shown that black pupils are more likely to be criticised and punished than pupils of other ethnic groups. Gillborn and Gipps (1996) report that the situation has changed little:

> ... irrespective of the teacher's conscious desire to help all pupils equally, the level of teacher–pupil conflict in the researched schools was such that, as a group, black pupils experienced school in ways that were significantly more conflictual and less positive than their peers. Teachers and schools may play an active, though unintended, role in the creation of conflict with African–Caribbean pupils, thereby reducing their opportunity to achieve. (p.55)

Mac an Ghiall (1989) takes this analysis further in his work on re-conceptualising black students' schooling experience. He notes that racist abuse and harassment may vary in different schools and localities, and teacher stereotyping of black pupils may vary according to pupil, age, social class and distribution of the ethnic minority group. But black communities are seen as problems, ethnicity is seen as a handicap to their assimilation or integration into British society. African–Caribbean educational failure or under-achievement is seen in terms of pathological structure of African–Caribbean family and kinship organisation. This was a view put forward in the Swann Report (DES 1985), but undermined by Wright (1986) in her ethnographic study of black pupils in three secondary schools, where she illustrated how the structures and processes of the schools themselves disadvantaged black pupils. In addition, McIntyre (1995) shows how pastoral care systems in secondary schools fail to support African–Caribbean pupils. He found a tendency for teachers to see black pupils more negatively, as less motivated and more likely to succeed in sports, music or social activities rather than academic work. Black pupils perceived teachers as less supportive and failing to deal with racism in schools. McIntyre noted that schools were less likely to involve black parents in a partnership to help solve problems experienced by their children, even though black parents appear to have more positive attitudes to their children's education than white parents.

The pervasiveness of racism (immigration, law, housing, employment, media) is taken for granted by black people living in Britain, but rarely acknowledged by white people. Black working class pupils give up in a racially stratified society with little contact between black and white. Contacts with whites tend to be with authority figures – teachers, careers officers and police. The number of black people working within the education service is much lower than would be predicted from the number of black people living in Britain. In September 1988 Ealing set up an independent enquiry into recruitment and promotion of ethnic minority teachers. Out of 140 new posts created only 3 went to ethnic minority teachers. Although 50 per cent of pupils in Ealing schools were of minority ethnic origin, only 8 per cent of teachers were black.

Olomolaiye (1995), writing of his experiences as a black educational psychologist, makes similar points. He comments that previous experiences may lead black people to be suspicious of the motives of the white people around them, especially authority figures such as the police, teachers and psychologists. He goes on to list some of the points that he encounters frequently which cause dissatisfaction amongst black parents when dealing with school:

• Being given insufficient information about their child's school work.
• Teachers being negative about their child.
• Threatening to exclude the child if parents do not agree to referral to a psychologist.
• Racism in the application of school rules – hairstyle and shoes being common examples.
• Not providing support in school for learning difficulties.

Again, what comes out of all these studies is the need for professional groups to be more active in recruiting black workers into their professions, and to be more willing to look at how they can improve liaison with black parents and black community groups in order to be aware of parental views, and make partnership a reality.

Values in special education

A main focus of debate in recent months has been the extent to which British society has fractured into many sub-groups, each having very different attitudes, beliefs and values with regard to a variety of moral and social issues. In mainstream education selection by ability, school uniforms, punishment, homework, the role of schools in spiritual and moral development, and even teaching methods themselves have all been seen as points of tension, with a variety of opinions held on each of these topics. The disagreements are not just between the major participants in the education system – pupils, parents, teachers, governors and politicians – as a range of values and opinions will be found in each of these groups. It has proved difficult to agree an overall and coherent set of values which can justify policy and practice in these areas at all levels of education.

Is education about providing for the development of individuals, of society and the state, with increasing equality of opportunities together with social cohesion and inclusion? Are SEN about what is additional and different from mainstream education, a specialisation with obvious benefits to the pupils? Or do they arise from the inability of mainstream education to include and provide for all learners? (See Norwich 1996.) Integration or segregation, inclusion or exclusion are the core concepts in this debate in the field of SEN.

Changes in the last two decades have seen the main focus of special education move from segregation to integration, and more recently to inclusive education. This view is not shared by two of the union leaders in relation to the closure of The Ridings school in Calderdale in November 1996: 'The real issue is about children who should be removed from mainstream to special schools where they could receive the education they need' and 'It is the closure of these schools (segregated special) which needs to be challenged, and the integration into mainstream school of children with serious behavioural problems'. (*Guardian* 4 November 1996.)

In trying to reconcile these different values and perspectives on SEN, Norwich (1996) suggests three kinds of special educational need:

• Those unique to an individual and different from all other children.
• Those common to all children (such as the need to belong, to feel loved, to feel related to others).
• Those exceptional needs arising from characteristics shared by some others (such as an emotional difficulty, visual impairment or giftedness).

This classification system does not address directly those differences that arise out of cultural values and beliefs, such as spiritual or religious values, or the importance of mother tongue, which will be common to a group and influence concepts such as the need to belong or to feel related to others. These are of key importance in whether individuals and groups from ethnic minorities will develop affiliation to the school as an institution and whether they will trust educational professionals to make decisions in the best interests of their children.

Special educational needs – differing perspectives

If mainstream schools decide they are not capable of meeting the particular needs of ethnic minority pupils because of factors arising out of linguistic, cultural or religious factors, they are likely to construe the problem in terms of learning difficulties, and use the special needs system as a way of getting resources, either to support the pupil in mainstream, or to find a segregated placement. Parents will see this as school rejecting their child and as institutional racism on the part of the education system in failing to provide appropriate schooling for their children.

In an attempt to clarify some of these difficulties, Adelman (1992) conceptualises special educational needs along a continuum ranging from type 1 problems (where causes are essentially located in the environment), through type 2 problems (resulting from an interaction between environment and the individual), to type 3 problems (where the cause is essentially intrinsic to the individual). This framework is particularly helpful in making sense of the findings reported above. There is unlikely to be any difficulty in identifying and reaching agreement between parents and professionals about the SEN of black pupils with severe and complex learning difficulties, physical disabilities and profound sensory impairments, all type 3 problems (although there may well still be differences in how to meet these special educational needs in terms of segregation or inclusion). The difficulties are with the type 1 and type 2 problems where parents, teachers, and other professionals may take very different views about the role played by the functioning of the school and its failure to meet the needs of individual pupils, rather than seeing difficulties as arising out of individual pupil problems.

Although the 1993 Education Act and the resulting Code of Practice place a great deal of emphasis on parental participation, and parent–professional partnership (see Chapter 10), the reality of power differentials often leaves parents feeling as though they are passive participants in the processes of identifying SEN and reaching decisions about provision. The experiences of black parents and communities, together with the knowledge and experiences of how the education system fails black pupils, adds a further dimension to the way problems will be seen.

Choudhury (1986) notes that the language and cultural differences, together with overt racism, may leave parents from ethnic minority communities confused and powerless when talking with teachers about issues such as SEN. A study by Rehal (1989) has shown how children may be placed in special schools while their parents remain unaware that an assessment of special educational needs has taken place, let alone having been given the opportunity to contribute to it. Caesar (1993) highlights the frequency with which professionals mishandle telling black parents that their child has a disability, the lack of support and information for black parents with pre-school children, inadequate home–school liaison, and the failure of services to address actively issues of racism and ethnicity as they affect service delivery to black clients. The involvement of black professionals and better liaison with the wider black community would help overcome these difficulties.

Segregated provision for pupils with SEN can be seen in different ways, depending on the belief and value systems held. Removing individuals from mainstream schools or classes is not merely socially divisive, restricting friendship groups, it also severely limits opportunities by restricting access to the curriculum, the examination system, further and higher education, and later employment opportunities. On the other hand, barring access to segregated provision on the basis of a value system emphasising inclusion can deprive children of the specialised curriculum they need.

The effect of different value systems can be seen clearly in the appeals procedures under the 1993 Education Act. Since independent tribunals for appeals against LEA decisions were set up, 40 per cent have been in the area of Special Learning Difficulties (SpLD) or dyslexia (Special Educational Needs Tribunal 1996). Although there are no figures on ethnicity provided in the Tribunal's Annual Report, one interpretation of the results is that mainly white, middle class parents are seeing the system as one which ensures they get additional resources for their children to help them overcome difficulties with the acquisition of literacy skills. These parents construe the SEN system as having resources which will enable their children to enhance their attainments, mainly through additional help in mainstream schools, but also by placement in specialist segregated schools. Parents of children with physical disabilities or with autism often seek segregated placements for similar reasons. This is in marked contrast to many ethnic minority groups.

Ng (1992) found many Chinese parents would be embarrassed or humiliated if segregated education was suggested. Many black parents and community groups, especially African–Caribbean, consider the special education system has been used to label black children inappropriately as having learning difficulties because of failures of the mainstream school system. This, together with exclusions and poorer exam results reinforce their views that schools have operated in such a way as to diminish, rather than enhance, educational opportunities and development. The SEN system is seen as yet another way of disadvantaging black children.

For example, Fish (1985) surveyed parents from different ethnic groups on their views on the special education provision made for their children. He found that African–Caribbean parents were significantly less happy with the special educational provision made for their children. They considered they had been insufficiently informed prior to their child's admission to special provision (42% as compared with 13% of other parents), and displeased with the decision to place their child in the present school (38% as compared with 12%). What was less clear from the survey is what forms of support would be more acceptable to these parents.

It is within this framework that black parents make sense of what is happening to their children, a system that so rarely acknowledges the particular needs of members of minority ethnic groups, and one where there are so few black professionals.

Spiritual and humanistic values

It is difficult to describe and understand the beliefs and attitudes of different groups in the area of special educational needs within the context of a class-based society in which disability, race and gender elicit a variety of perspectives which interact with each other. Individuals will adopt different coping and survival strategies linked to their own core values, which in turn will link in with those of the wider religious, ethnic and secular communities that influence their lives.

Within Britain there is a variety of views of disability that link with particular religious, spiritual or secular beliefs. There is, for example, the view held by the major religious groups – Christian, Muslim and Hindu – that children with severe mental disability are incapable of doing wrong, and therefore close to God. Many religious groups would share this perspective, which informs views on the acceptance of disability and how it might help carers of disabled children and adults. A secular stance is becoming more common, with the notion that professional intervention, based on science and technology, offers different ways of responding to disability. If disability can be detected during gestation then abortion may be an option for parents to consider. When disability is diagnosed after birth, the difficulty may be in accepting the limitations of intervention, and the fact that a cure is impossible. Much emotional energy may be spent on seeking out experts who will give them a 'normal child'.

There are differences between ethnic groups and the range of religious, spiritual or secular views that are likely to be held. The danger is that professionals may feel that they can move from these generalisations to 'know' what particular parents may believe and value. The work cited above emphasises the need for professionals to be sensitive to the views of individuals, and not to impose their own stereotyped views of particular religious or ethnic groups onto individual parents.

Responding to the special educational needs of black pupils – the SUMES project

Some LEAs have tried to address these issues in an attempt to enable the education system to meet the educational needs of black pupils. In response to the concerns of black parents, professionals and communities, Sheffield Unified Multicultural Education Service (SUMES) was set up in January 1987 to provide a coherent educational service to black children and adults. The broad remit of the unified service was made clear in its statement of aims and objectives which included:

- to contribute to a more accountable education service by listening to and consulting with black parents and communities to identify and respond to needs.
- to provide direct support to black pupils and students in education, and to enhance ways in which black communities contribute to the education service
- to develop new ideas that will improve educational access for black people
- to develop new and more relevant educational services for Sheffield's black communities.

As well as providing direct linguistic, curricular and cultural support to all black pupils in the city, SUMES celebrates black contributions to British cultural life, improves access to educational services and employs black staff. Systems have been developed to provide any necessary professional training for the individuals recruited into the service.

There is a tendency in education to substitute much needed action with lengthy discussions about race and racism awareness. Gurnah (1992) suggests that direct action and targeting of resources are the ways to increase learning opportunities for black people, and this view of targeting resources has been the major strategy of SUMES in the field of SEN, helping mainstream and special schools to meet the special educational needs of pupils from the black communities. This has led to the development of a special educational needs team within SUMES, comprising an educational psychologist, teachers and non-teaching assistants. Although the team works cooperatively to ensure a planned delivery of service, each professional group has a different role.

As well as working with SUMES, colleagues, and with groups within a number of black communities, the educational psychologist also has a generic role working in schools with significant numbers of black pupils. Additionally there is consultative work with colleagues within the educational psychology service, to help them improve their work in the identification, assessment and intervention of black pupils with SEN.

The special needs team now has a coordinator, six support teachers (two secondary, two primary, one under fives and one for hearing impaired pupils) together with ten non-teaching assistants. This team deals with a wide range of SEN – communication and language impairments, hearing or visual impairments, physical disabilities, emotional or behavioural difficulties as well as mild to severe learning difficulties. In many cases the issues of identification, assessment and intervention are complicated by the fact that English is a second language for many pupils. The team is not only aware of these issues, but in many cases there are members who share the community language and cultural values of their client group, and are thus better able to relate to children and parents. The effect of SUMES has been to recruit more black teachers into the education system and, if necessary help black people gain the qualifications needed to fulfil the required roles in the system. Moreover, several of these staff have moved into senior positions in other parts of the LEA – headteachers, advisers and senior managers – providing greater expertise throughout the system in the particular needs of black children and improving communication with black parents and community groups .

Evaluations of SUMES have been positive (SUMES review report 1993), and a start has been made in helping the education system become more responsive to the needs and aspirations of black students, their families and communities in both mainstream and special education.

Conclusion

Values in special education are intimately related to the value systems held by the major participants in the mainstream system – teachers, education officers, governors, politicians and parents. The perceptions of parents from ethnic minority communities are shaped by the degree to which the mainstream system has, over the last thirty years, failed to offer equal opportunities for their children. Examination results have been poorer and the major educational reforms of the 1980s, including the national curriculum, have not taken account of the changes and trends in British society leading towards cultural pluralism. Few members of ethnic minority communities have been recruited to professional groups or political parties, and the particular needs of pupils from ethnic minority groups have been neglected by the education system.

Although the concept of special needs is complex, and open to different interpretations, the three categories suggested by Adelman form a useful framework to consider how conflicts may arise, especially over type 1 and type 2 problems, which are caused by difficulties within the educational environment, or from an interaction between the individual and the educational environment. But many ethnic minority groups see little reason to trust white educational professionals or the education system to reach decisions that are in the best interests of their children. Institutional racism and individual racism are further factors influencing ethnic minority groups to treat with caution interventions of professionals in their lives. All these are potent forces shaping their value systems.

Although we group a variety of very different ethnic communities as 'ethnic minority groups', there are real and very important differences between and within them. Professionals need to be sensitive to these differences, as well as to the commonly held beliefs and values which unite these groups; to put aside stereotypic views of particular groups, and develop ways of working which enable them to listen to the views of individual parents; and to develop a meaningful partnership with them, and ensure the education system meets the needs of their child. The experience of SUMES is that using democratic processes which tap into community structures ensures voices can be heard and the system can be sensitive to them.

It is likely that developing partnership in this way will reveal a range of values around special education provision, requiring a heterogeneous system. Some parents will argue strongly for inclusive education, with their child being placed in the local school and supported there. Others will value integrated provision allowing some specialist provision such as buildings suitable for wheelchair access or facilities and teachers for pupils with significant hearing impairments. Finally, some may feel that segregated provision is the best way of meeting the special educational needs of their child. Working in partnership with parents and community groups from ethnic minorities means politicians and professionals have to create a climate of trust, where policy development and implementation takes account of the diverse value systems present in their local communities. An approach to special education that results in a homogeneous system is unlikely to meet the aspirations of many minority groups. Equal opportunity policies should ensure high quality service delivery to all groups, as well as the recruitment of members of ethnic minority groups into the education profession; teachers, psychologists and administrators.

Acknowledgements

My thanks to Dr. Ahmed Gurnah and Dr. F'Oluso Olomolaiye for commenting on early drafts of this chapter. This chapter is dedicated to my son Joseph, who has taught me so much about racism.

Chapter 4

Values of Professional Groups Dealing with Children with Special Educational Needs

Ingrid Lunt

Introduction

A large number of professionals from the health, education, social services, and other backgrounds, work with children with special educational needs. The values expressed by these different individuals and groups reflect their professional background, their individual experience, and the context in which they live and work. Professional values may accord or conflict with personal values, and it is essential that both professionals and their clients are aware of this. It is also very important to be aware that both professional and personal values are substantially influenced by current society and its values. Society reflects and creates strong value positions, as do institutions.

Professionals do not operate in a value-free or value-neutral vacuum. For example, our society now is very different from what it was 10 or 20 years ago, with fewer certainties and less consensus over values; views which may have been unthinkable even 10 years ago may now be fairly acceptable or even commonplace. Education provides a particular example of a context where very different values are demonstrated in practice; although these values depend substantially on views of the kind of society that we wish to live in, education forms the meeting point for very different values which may co-exist or be juxtaposed. There are inevitably tensions between value positions concerning individual excellence versus collective benefit, and between progressive notions of equality of opportunity and more conservative ideals of individual fulfilment and elitism, and differing views on the 'best' contribution to society. The title of a recent book '*All Must have Prizes*' (Phillips 1997) demonstrates a fundamental tension in educational philosophy. Indeed, as Norwich suggests:

> there is no overall and coherent set of values which can justify policy and practice at all levels in education ... no single and exclusive value or principle, whether it be equality or individuality or social inclusion, can encompass what is commonly considered to be worthwhile. (Norwich 1996, p.100)

This chapter will focus mainly on the welfare state professionals concerned with special education, and attached to the special education sections of LEAs: administrators, advisers and inspectors, heads of specialist support teaching services and, in particular, educational psychologists, a group of professionals collectively referred to by Lipsky as 'street level bureaucrats' (Lipsky 1980). It will first consider the context of special education and some of the tensions and conflicts inherent in the field of special educational needs. The context for thinking about values in special education reflects changes in society in general, which are in turn dependent on political, economic, ideological and social influences. The field of special education, and its values, have been significantly affected by changes in legislation in education over the past 20 years; in particular the recent introduction of a market orientation with notions of consumerism and choice into this field, have created a very different context for professionals whose practice was informed by the development of the field of 'special educational needs' (SEN) in the late 1970s and early 1980s. The chapter then considers the professionals working in the field and their professional values. Some of their conflicts are illustrated through examples of two case studies.

Themes and value positions in Special Education

A number of themes which reflect the development of different value positions are evident through a brief history of special education. Developments in educational practices are the product of a complex interplay between social and political values, the 'needs' of society, current educational orthodoxy, the views and values of professionals, parents and increasingly young people themselves, and other influences. Professionals and their values are heavily influenced by the ideology of the day.

'Benevolent humanitarianism'

Early provision for pupils with special needs began in the eighteenth century through charitable initiatives; this was segregated provision. Claimed to be motivated by notions of caring and protection, and referred to as 'benevolent humanitarianism' (Tomlinson 1982), special education also served as a 'safety valve' for ordinary schools, enabling them to function without those pupils whose presence was difficult to accommodate. It also reflected the values of the time and enabled professionals to identify, place and provide for pupils who were judged not able to fit into the ordinary school system. Professionals, particularly medical professionals, had complete power and were considered to be the unchallengeable experts and to 'know best'. The apparent rationality of professional judgements concerning the placement and segregation of pupils who did not fit in, reflected clear views about the nature of society, and the authority of professionals.

Classification and categorisation

The 11 categories of handicap in the 1945 Regulations following the 1944 Education Act formalised professionals' ability to secure additional resources for children with SEN by categorising, labelling and segregation, informed by a medical view and locating the origins of difficulties within the child, and placing them in special schools. Decisions over placement were left to the professionals who claimed some 'scientific' objectivity and accuracy in their judgements of children's abilities, and who justified the segregated placements by claims of 'what is best for the child'. Thus, Skrtic refers to the four grounding assumptions of special education:

* Disabilities are pathological conditions that students have
* Differential diagnosis is objective and useful
* Special education is a rationally conceived and coordinated system of services that benefits diagnosed students
* Progress results from incremental technological improvements in diagnosis and instructional interventions. (Skrtic 1991, p.54)

The system was justified by a value system based on rationality, positivism, scientific evidence, and professional hegemony. However, while some disabilities may be relatively appropriately approached in this way, at least in initial stages, Tomlinson has suggested that there are other categories of SEN, in particular moderate learning difficulties and emotional and behavioural difficulties, which are socially constructed by the decisions and beliefs of professional people, while serving the wider social purpose of removing potentially troublesome children (Tomlinson 1982). According to this view, while under the guise of individual self-fulfilment, special education is more about social control and engineering.

Equal opportunities and human rights

The 'integration' movements of the 1970s which spread across western countries coincided with societal and to an extent professional concerns with human rights and equal opportunities which were ideological in nature and driven by a particular set of values, in particular a shift from concepts of compassion and charity to rights and opportunities. At the same time client groups were becoming mobilised and demanding their rights to equal opportunity. Thus, across the western world, countries were passing forms of integration legislation and in the United Kingdom, the Warnock Report (Department of Education and Science 1978) and the 1981 Education Act embodied the principles of integration. The Report and the legislation were introduced into a climate of general egalitarian and expansionist values of the late 1970s, and a general impetus across the western world towards greater equality, in particular for disabled and disadvantaged members of society. In addition, members of such disadvantaged groups were themselves acquiring a voice, and beginning to express their own views as to entitlement and equality.

Integration versus segregation

Integration is a topic associated with deeply felt emotions and heated debates which raise questions about the nature of society, how to deal with difference and diversity and basic values relating to the nature and purposes of education. On the one side are those with an ideological commitment to an inclusive system of education which meets the needs of all pupils whatever their ability or disability. Many 'disabled' groups fall into this category. On the other hand are those with an equally strong ideological commitment to individuality and choice, to pupils' rights to a different education according to their different needs and abilities. Many 'disabled' groups fall into this category. These very different positions reflect different value positions. Cutting across both positions is the administrative position which requires consideration of 'efficient use of resources' and possible 'economies of scale'. In addition, Barton and Tomlinson suggest that:

> integration is not solely the product of benevolent and enlightened attitudes to children. The motives behind integration, just as those behind segregation, are a product of complex social, economic and political considerations which may relate more to the 'needs' of the wider society, the whole education system and professionals working within the system rather than simply to the 'needs' of individual children. (Barton and Tomlinson 1984, p.65)

Administrative decisions about integration are thus influenced by pragmatic concerns and finance, and the conflicts in ideological position concerning integration and inclusive education lead to many decisions being influenced by subjective value positions as well as practical factors.

Choice and diversity

Recent education legislation and developments, beginning with the 1988 Education Reform Act, continuing with the White Paper *Choice and Diversity* (Department for Education 1992), and the 1993 Education Act, and reflected in the recent 1996 and forthcoming 1997 Education Acts, reflect a world-wide influence of 'the market' and the values associated with this approach, along with the introduction of 'new managerialism' to many areas of the public sector. 'Choice', 'diversity', 'competition' and 'consumerism' along with 'accountability', 'performance indicators', 'league tables' and 'value for money' reflect the policies and values of a society which appears to be increasingly pursuing educational excellence and individualism at the cost of equality and social inclusion. (See also Chapter 2 for a further discussion.)

Thus we can see that the present social climate and context is a very different one from that of the late 1970s and early 1980s when the concept of 'special educational needs' was introduced into an expansionist educational culture, which embraced relatively inclusive and egalitarian values. It is suggested that this fact may pose particular dilemmas and conflicts for professionals working in this area.

Tensions and dilemmas within special education

It will be apparent that conflict is inherent in the whole process of special education and dealing with the diversity of pupils' needs. Conflict arises at the ideological, the philosophical, the administrative, the organisational and the practical level. It concerns, amongst other issues, questions about the goals of education, approaches to pupils' diversity, views about the nature and purposes of 'ordinary' schools, and about how educational resources should be shared. Conflict arises also when the climate of legislation changes, as for example, when the social welfare model of the 1970s on which the Warnock recommendations were based, proves incompatible with a philosophy of economic and social individualism of the late 1980s and the 1990s. All of these involve value positions. It is possible to pose a number of questions within special education:

- What kind of schools do we want? Whose needs should 'ordinary' schools meet? Can effective schools be totally inclusive?
- Are the goals of education the same for all pupils and should they all be entitled to participate in the same schools the same curriculum and the same activities? If they are (as stated in the Warnock Report 1978), how can these be realised?
- Who needs or deserves additional resources? Should resources go to the most needy and the most deserving, or those that might most benefit, or most contribute given additional resources?
- Whose best interests should be taken into consideration? Should schools consider first the needs of individual pupils, the needs of the majority of pupils, the needs of teachers, the needs of parents, or, indeed, the needs of professionals?
- How do we protect provision for individual pupils while also avoiding the stigma of identification and labelling?

As described by Pumfrey (1996) decision makers in special education face several conflicting issues: resources are finite, priorities contentious, knowledge is partial and demands are infinite. Professionals in special education have the task and responsibility of making judgements about the needs of another person, and of making decisions which may significantly affect that other person's life and life chances. These professional judgements will be influenced by professionals' values. 'An overarching ideology, or generalised belief, that unites all the professionals, is that whatever they do will be acting 'in the best interests of the child.' (Galloway *et al.* 1994, p.119.) However, even this may not always be possible, since professionals wishing to make decisions based on their professional and personal judgements of the needs of the child may be put under pressure by their employers to make recommendations which are affordable by the LEA, thus highlighting the constraints and role ambiguity of this group of professionals.

Professionals working in special education

Following the 1981 Education Act, 'special educational needs' became professionalised and special education professionals proliferated both in number and in type. Although the government of the day did not allocate additional resources for the implementation of the 1981 Act, LEAs themselves spent substantially more on special education, creating a new group of professionals such as special needs advisers, special needs advisory teachers, support teachers, special needs administrators and so on (Goacher *et al.* 1988). The number of educational psychologists increased considerably, in part because of their statutory role in the formal assessment process. In 1983 we saw the development of courses for teachers in mainstream schools, predecessors of SENCOs (Cowne and Norwich 1987) and the formal emergence of the SEN professional within mainstream schools. Speech therapists took on an educational role in addition to their medical focus, and other professionals became drawn into the group of special education professionals through the multi-professional collaboration advocated by the Warnock Report and the 1981 Education Act.

The suggestion that significant numbers of children in mainstream schools had special educational needs (Warnock's '18 per cent') thus led to increasing numbers of professionals operating outside schools, and laying claim to expert knowledge in respect of children's special needs. This in turn probably played a part in encouraging the notion in schools that certain children were 'someone else's problem' or the illusion that only specialists could handle these kind of children, and to ever larger numbers of children being identified as 'different' i.e. as having special needs of some kind, and being in need of 'professional' help.

These developments resulted in a raised awareness of the issue of SEN and an enhanced status for SEN professionals, but this professionalisation also brought with it many of the disadvantages of a model and the values of 'expertise' or 'specialism'. 'The very nature of professionalisation makes professionals susceptible to the delusion that their knowledge tradition and its associated practices and discourses are objective and inherently correct' (Skrtic 1991, p.85). This brings with it a further assumption that professionals will by definition and without question be acting in the best interests of the child, and that their decisions are objective and rational.

The professions have traditionally enjoyed a privileged position, gaining the trust of clients and community in exchange for their claims to expert knowledge and integrity. Thus, traditionally, professionals were trusted to know best, their judgement was not questioned, and it was assumed that they would be acting in the best interests of their clients and according to some 'objective' and 'rational' expertise, and operating in a value-neutral context. Although it is clear that welfare state professionals within the education system such as special education professionals are not operating in this 'traditional' manner, and as employees within the state sector are probably more like Etzioni's 'semi-professionals', the role ambiguity posed by the situation may nevertheless and perhaps particularly lead to value conflicts.

The fundamental role of the LEA is to identify pupils whose needs cannot be met through generally available provision (i.e. by schools through their delegated budgets) and to ensure that additional or different provision is made. This role is passed on by the LEA to its special education professionals whose task in turn is to identify pupils in need of additional resources, a largely administrative task. These professionals:

> have (or appear to have) considerable discretion over the allocation of resources for particular groups of children deemed to have 'special needs'. Whilst this exercise of discretion gives the street level bureaucrat considerable power, it is accompanied by the need to operate adequately in a situation where resources are constrained and limited. This results in many street level bureaucrats acting as gatekeepers to relatively powerless groups. Their task is to manage and restrict demand on resources according to often submerged criteria ... Thus 'need' is determined by subjective factors and judgements, which are then presented as objective. (Vincent *et al.* 1996, p. 477)

This highlights a powerful conflict and ambiguity within the professional role, for example, between the professional judgement that a pupil needs additional resources, and the awareness that the LEA does not have these resources, a conflict which is only exacerbated by recourse to the tribunals set up under the 1993 Education Act. Thus the illusion that it is possible to quantify need 'scientifically' and objectively provides a justification for both administrative and judicial decisions which make it difficult for LEAs to plan policy according to principles of equity. However, as Armstrong (1995) has pointed out, there are increasing contradictions for professionals between 'professional services performed on behalf of clients and bureaucratic functions performed on behalf of the state' (p.138). For example, an educational psychologist makes an assessment of a child and forms a judgement that the child needs additional resources; the LEA has over-spent its budget and has placed a limit on the number of statements. Or, to take another example, two children aged 12 have a measured reading age of 8: one child has a measured IQ of 120, while that of the other child is 80; which child has the greater 'need' or is more 'deserving' of additional resources? A third example illustrates a further conflict of values: an educational psychologist judges that a 'gifted' child is more deserving of additional resources than a child with learning difficulties, since the former is more able to benefit from the resources, while a colleague takes the opposite view, having a commitment to compensating for social disadvantage. In addition, educational psychologists have their own personal values, influencing their views on human nature, the nature and purpose of education, and their attitudes to diversity.

> Faced with the scale and complexity of urban industrial society, the state looks to the technical expertise offered by the professions. This has the additional ideological advantage of enabling the state to present essentially political questions as technical and value-free. (Cole and Furbey 1994, p.130)

Professional Codes of Ethics

A traditional defining feature of professionals is adherence to a code of ethics and disciplinary procedures administered by the professional body or association. In this section reference is made to the professional bodies of educational psychologists as an example.

Both the Association of Educational Psychologists' Code of Professional Practice and that of the British Psychological Society Division of Educational and Child Psychology open with the clause:

> Educational psychologists aim to protect the welfare of any person who may seek their service or be the subject of their study. They shall not use their professional position or relationships nor shall they knowingly permit their services or knowledge to be used by others for purposes inconsistent with this aim (BPS, DECP 1995).

Guidelines for clinical psychologists produced by the British Psychological Society's Division of Clinical Psychology have a similar clause:

> The work of a clinical psychologist is based on the fundamental acknowledgement that all people have the same human value and the right to be treated as unique individuals. (BPS, DCP 1994)

These are laudable value positions. Although the question of who is the educational psychologist's client is much debated, and educational psychologists have simultaneously to hold responsibilities to different clients, they often see themselves primarily as providing a service to children and their families. Head teachers often consider that educational psychologists are providing a service to schools, and of course the LEA expects that educational psychologists are providing a service to the LEA in assisting it to make decisions about the allocation of additional resources for SEN. This role ambiguity and overlap in client responsibilities gets to the heart of some of the value conflicts for professional educational psychologists.

> If educational psychologists were only accountable to children and parents, the nature of their role might perhaps be negotiated and clarified without undue difficulty. The reality is that they are caught in a complex web in which the interests of their secondary clients, namely teachers and other LEA officers, are dictated by wider considerations arising from muddle and confusion in government policy. (Galloway *et al.* 1994, p.101)

In human services there may be an inevitable clash between professional values and the constraints of the system; there may also be a clash between the institutional values, individual professional values and the professional's personal values.

Professional values

Professional values are not time and context free, and are strongly influenced by societal and political values and ideologies (Lindsay 1995). Nevertheless, there are many professionals who claim to be operating value-free and neutral and, as Skrtic (1991) implies, in an objective manner which transcends personal values. Professionals acquire the trust of clients through their expertise, their presumed altruism and concern for their clients' good, and their adherence to codes of conduct: 'armed with their expert knowledge, professionals ask to be trusted and do not expect their clients to question their judgements' (Galloway *et al.* 1994, p.123). The past decade has witnessed growing criticism of professionals, and the growth of a culture of 'anti-professionalism'. Part of this results from pressures for accountability and openness: 'it is not good enough (for professionals) to rest on (their) roles as 'experts'. Professionals have a duty to be open and accountable, to enable clients to understand (their) interventions and to engage in an informed manner in decision-making' (Lindsay, op cit, p.495). Such pressures lead to welcome developments in improved communication, less use of jargon, and greater partnership.

There is another way in which professional values are increasingly put to the test in relation to work in the human services. Newnes (1996) suggests that 'the stated purpose and values of the profession may not match the values or practice of its practitioners who might themselves have difficulty in articulating personal values'. He calls for professionals to articulate their real values and 'see through the homogenising culture of our profession' (that of clinical psychology). Examples which may provoke mixed feelings, based on value conflict, may include work with clients with strong racist or sexist beliefs, particular religious beliefs, or particular values in relation to lifestyle. In these situations it is essential that the professional be aware of personal values and the extent to which these may be influencing the professional interaction and work. In relation to work in the field of SEN, the professional's own educational experience, and own personal beliefs about inclusion, segregation, specialisation, elitism, and entitlement are likely to influence their professional stance, and their own experience of and attitude to authority may affect their professional behaviour. This is particularly important to take into consideration when training professionals to work in the field.

Case examples

The following cases are based on real pupils, though some details have been changed.

Case 1

Tom is a ten year old in Year 6 who finds school difficult to handle. He is very large for his age, has a lot of energy and aggression, and is boisterous in his dealings with other children and with teachers. He seeks adult attention continuously, and is becoming increasingly violent in his attempts to secure his teachers' time and attention. He is continually out of his seat, prodding other children with a ruler, tearing up bits of paper and latterly books, disrupting activities, and upsetting arrangements such as plants, displays and artwork. Although he is approaching Key Stage 2 assessment, his work is more like that of children at Key Stage 1.

A succession of teachers at the school have put up with this behaviour which has deteriorated over the past three years. The head teacher now considers that the mainstream school is no longer able to meet his needs. She feels that she needs to protect the teachers in her school. Tom's parents wish him to remain at the school and to continue on to the local comprehensive school with his friends. His father, in particular, considers that the school has not been strong enough in its discipline, and that it is the fault of the school that Tom is 'a little boisterous'. Tom also wishes to go on to the local comprehensive. The LEA has recently disbanded a behaviour support service which used to go into schools to work with pupils having similar difficulties to Tom. There is, however, a Pupil Referral Unit (PRU) locally which takes pupils for short periods with a view to return to mainstream school.

The educational psychologist has observed Tom over the course of the school year. She realises that Tom's difficulties have become exacerbated partly by two other boys who tease him mercilessly about his size, and partly by the teacher who has confessed that she cannot handle him and has taken a dislike to him. The class has already had two teachers this school year. The educational psychologist believes strongly that schools should be inclusive, and she has worked over time with the schools in her area to try to achieve this.

During a meeting with the teachers and Tom's parents, the conflict in values and views becomes clear. The teachers have reached a stage where they wish to exclude Tom, stating that the needs of the other children must be taken into consideration and that Tom needs specialist help and separate provision. The head teacher supports this position thinking of the needs of the staff. The parents are adamant that Tom should not be assessed for possible special school placement. The educational psychologist respects this view, believing that Tom should remain in mainstream school and that she should be working in partnership with the parents whose views should be respected. She feels that the school could do a lot to help Tom and that he has not been given a fair chance. There is a place at the PRU and the head teacher believes that it would be best for Tom and for the other pupils and teachers at the school if he were to transfer to the PRU at least for the remainder of his time in Junior School.

* The parents believe that Tom has not been given a fair chance. They consider that the school is too lax in discipline.
* The educational psychologist believes that much of Tom's difficulties are influenced by the school, its pattern of pastoral care and discipline; she also believes strongly in an inclusive system of schooling. She identifies with Tom and his family (like Tom, she is also mixed-race), and she finds the head teacher somewhat rigid.
* The teachers feel unsupported and over-stressed. They believe that children with SEN, particularly behaviour difficulties, need specialist help in a separate school.

This case could escalate into a situation where the school excludes Tom, and where the people involved become polarised in their views. The parents refuse a statutory assessment, the school refuses to accommodate Tom, and Tom is unable to change his behaviour.

Case 2

Maria is an eleven year old in Year 7 who has just started at her local comprehensive school: she has a severe visual impairment which is progressive; she has lost the sight in one eye, and has only residual vision in the other eye. She is very shy and withdrawn, and received a lot of support within the classroom at her junior school, although her parents would not allow any professionals other than her teachers to work with her. The family moved to this country five years ago, and have a deep distrust of all professionals. They do not acknowledge the severity of Maria's difficulties, and believe that she can cope with ordinary school provided she wears her spectacles and sits at the front of the class. They are adamant that she will not have a statutory assessment, and that no specialists may come into contact with her.

At school Maria is increasingly vulnerable, the size and busyness of the comprehensive school being very different from the smaller school on one level where she has survived for the past five years. She is at risk of being knocked over by other pupils, and has become increasingly withdrawn. She is becoming very behind in her work, and her one haven appears to be the art room where she produces some fine artwork after painstaking and extreme effort. The educational psychologist has observed her in class, but parents have withheld permission for any professional or specialist involvement.

- The parents distrust professionals and fear any form of specialist involvement.
- The teachers feel helpless, dislike the parents and believe that Maria should be in a special school for children with visual impairment.
- The specialist teacher for visual impairment also feels helpless and believes that pupils like Maria should be in mainstream school and are able to cope with the appropriate support and aids.
- The educational psychologist believes that all children with severe sensory impairment should go to special school where their needs may be met, and where they will be working with pupils with similar disabilities.
- The LEA has plans to cut the peripatetic service for visual impairment, and hopes to rationalise provision for this disability, making economies of scale, with a primary unit attached to a junior school, and provision for secondary pupils in a unit attached to a different comprehensive school some miles away.

The situation has reached an impasse, where the authority is placing increasing pressure on the family to permit specialist involvement and a statutory assessment. This raises questions of parents' rights, Maria's rights, and professionals' views about these and the role of the local authority in relation to care and the child's best interests.

Conclusions

The field of SEN challenges professional decision making and values. Professionals in the field of SEN have to be aware of several layers of value influences: first their own personal value positions, beliefs and personal ideologies; second the professional values which arise from their professional identity and their code of conduct; third the institutional values which permeate their place of work; and fourth the social values which are articulated more widely and which achieve acceptance as part of a wider educational culture. In practice, SEN professionals in the public sector are not able to exercise complete independence in their decision-making, and are always working within the framework of local constraints, both practical and financial. Decisions as to how to allocate additional resources, who deserves more, and how to meet pupils' diversity are inevitably influenced by a myriad of factors, including professional values and subjective judgements, and it is essential that professionals and their clients are aware of this fact.

Part 2

Values in Schools

Chapter 5

Values and Judgements of School Managers

David Thompson

Introduction – The voice of the head teacher

The purpose of this brief chapter is to hear the voices of some head teachers on the dilemmas they have to face, with their senior staff and special needs staff, on what arrangements to put in place to support the education of individual children with special needs. These voices are voices of mainstream school head teachers, both of primary and secondary schools, some with integrated units for children with special needs in their schools, and some without. In spite of the variety of their situations, they rarely disagreed with one another, the main differences being the particular priority they would give to questions of special needs provision in their school as compared with other demands.

There has been much discussion in the literature of the various systems for supporting children with special needs, particularly since the Code Of Practice (Department for Education 1994) became operational, including discussions of the role of the special needs coordinator (SENCO) in school, the special needs governor, classroom support assistants and other support staff. In the end, however, some of the critical decisions made by schools about the education of children with special needs involve the head teacher. The decisions are ones of critical importance for the children concerned: such as whether the school should accept or refuse entry to a child of given special needs; whether they should suspend or exclude a student because the school seemed to be making no impact on learning or behaviour; or whether the school should initiate a statutory assessment, with the explicit intention of finding more appropriate provision to meet these needs elsewhere, on the grounds that the student appeared to be making no progress in the present school. The head, of course, is not the only member of staff involved in these decisions, but is often seen to have a crucial influence on them, and these heads would accept that role and responsibility.

The first general point they all agreed on was that values held by staff were extremely important in their schools, and the heads tended to assume that the important values were the ones which they themselves more or less supported. Some of the heads had a sense of 'the school's community', by which they meant the particular sets of families and the particular geographical area from which the children attending their school came. The values that they thought important specifically include delivery of effective education to all children in the school, and being aware of the individual needs of all children, especially those who were 'needy'. One head encapsulated this neatly in the phrase 'it is very clear that those with the most need, need most', when referring to the claims on time and resources which individual children made. The heads saw these values as being a part of the school ethos, and some were quite explicit at saying they would use the criterion of expressing these particular values when selecting teachers at interview for posts in school.

This idea of valuing children – and also valuing staff – is one of the important issues in general management theory and practice (Day *et al.* 1993) and so possibly in expressing these views the heads were doing no more than following the orthodox line. However, all of them seem to have a very specific notion of the particular needs of the children they were talking about, and, in a wide divergence from the perspectives of most texts on school management, specifically did include children with special needs along with the other underachieving children in school, as well as children whom they saw as not having the best background to support effective learning in a school.

The small minority of children who would be expected to receive a statement of special educational needs were included in their general view of 'needy children', but the selection of which particular children would be able to 'achieve a statement' was seen as a relatively arbitrary process which by itself could not be trusted to indicate those with the greatest need. They were, however, quite clear that the mainstream school could not possibly meet all the needs of children by themselves – they needed the expertise and the resources from other parts of the education service, including the general resourcing power of the local education authority itself, as well as the specific expertise of support staff and of special schools and units.

One head with a particular pro-inclusion set of views did refer to the need for an 'ideological underpinning of inclusion'. He felt that the cases variously made for the attendance of children with special needs at mainstream schools were almost always made on the basis of parental choice or availability of provision, and the philosophical and moral arguments for inclusive education tended to be ignored.

The head and the staff

All the heads saw themselves as taking decisions alongside and on behalf of other involved staff within the school. Key persons in this group were the special needs coordinator, any other members of the senior management team particularly involved with special needs or pastoral care issues, the staff of any special units in school, and indeed the individual teachers who would be most implicated in teaching the child under consideration. In general, they described a human system of consultation and decision-making based round the perceived needs of individual students. The way in which the school's special needs policy related to the particular situation of the student being considered appeared only as a background issue. It appeared as though such policies only achieved their reality when they were translated into known procedures for supporting children and coming to decisions, such as a point at which parents became involved when developments occurred in children's education, or when policies were translated into the range of options for providing extra help and support for children in school. This kind of consultation with staff seemed to have an element of looking for the creative solution to emerging problems, of the type advocated by Torrington and Weightman (1989). For a child in school, the heads varied in the extent to which they saw themselves as being involved with children's progression through the Code Of Practice stages one to four. However, they distinctly gave the impression that if they were personally aware of a serious need on the part of the child one of their responses would be to 'argue for a statement of special educational needs' to support their staff, and also because they felt it was appropriate that extra resources were provided by the LEA.

The head as manager of an organisational system

All the heads constantly referred to the opinions of other interested parties, particularly teachers and parents of other children, although not ignoring the parents of the child whose needs were under consideration. They were also keenly aware of teachers' and parents' capabilities as primary carers to help the children. Community networks involving both professionals and non-educationists were much valued, as some parents of 'needy' children were seen as deserving particular support themselves from agencies including health visitors and the Education Welfare Service. The capabilities of the teaching staff involved were also taken very seriously. The teachers' efforts should be expended to good effect in terms of the children making progress, and also so that the teachers should not be over-taxed and unnecessarily stressed. The concerns of the heads were very clearly for the health and effectiveness of the organisation as a whole. They saw themselves as having a specifically managerial role in balancing costs and benefits across the system for all concerned.

Financial considerations

All the heads specifically mentioned that since the advent of local financial management (LMS) and even more so the implementation of the Code Of

Practice, the financial aspects of making provision for children with special educational needs had become much more important. One head felt that since these developments different kinds of special educational need had almost become a currency in themselves, having implications for management of staff resources. For example, should more staff salary budget be spent on classroom assistants to support children with special needs rather than replacing a teacher? There were implications for timetabling to make the best use of classroom assistants' time owing to the school containing a number of children with statements.

One head spoke very appreciatively of the extra resourcing which accrued to the school from the existence of its special unit, and how these budgetary implications had been a major factor in the success of his special needs policy over the years. When staff had realised the extent to which the local educational authority supported children with special needs financially, they had been much more willing to operate a general special needs policy stressing inclusion, and now many valued inclusion for its own sake and not only for the particular financial advantages. Another head described appreciatively how the minibus which was first acquired for the special needs unit was now also used by many other parts of the school. The financial backing for providing effective education for children with special needs was seen as a strong statement of the positive value which the wider community put on providing effective education for the various groups of disabled children. In turn the heads felt that they could influence the attitudes and practices of staff members through allocation of money and explicit recognition of the source of these extra resources of staff time and capitation.

Long-term policy considerations

Some of the heads who were particularly keen to operate effective policies of inclusion specifically mentioned aspects of long-term staff development policies which they saw as consolidating attitudes amongst their staff in favour of inclusive education. One head, for example, described how he was working towards achieving greater flexibility in staff deployment between staff who were habitually attached to the special unit and those teaching mainstream classes. He saw it as important that the staff in the mainstream classes had some experience of teaching children who were attached to the unit, and vice versa, to increase staff confidence in teaching right across the ability range. This should achieve effective differentiation of the curriculum, both for the children attached to the unit and those children who needed greater curriculum differentiation in the mainstream classes. Another head spoke of the school's participation in a rolling programme of training for classroom assistants to support mainstream teachers as effectively as possible in teaching children with special needs in their classes. This particular head also acknowledged that in some instances the effect of the training was that the classroom assistant had more knowledge of the child's special educational needs and the teaching approaches which were necessary than the subject teacher, and this pointed to the need for much greater training in special needs for many of the main scale staff in the school.

Impact of values on the key decisions

As indicated above, most heads specifically mentioned the decisions relating to special needs as being among the most stressful of the decisions which they commonly had to make. These included the admission, or not, of children with known special needs records, the suspension or exclusion of children from school often with some degree of special needs involvement in the broader definition of the term, and the process of achieving a statement, both to acquire any extra resources possible and to test out thoroughly if a child was correctly placed in this school. Views as to why this was so included statements such as:

> You know you are going to be seen as the big bad wolf if you say no, but you also know that being seduced into accepting or keeping a child in school when the school is not meeting their needs at all is a recipe for double trouble in the future.

> You usually end up having the deciding voice between two groups of people holding quite different views, the school staff on one hand and parents and external agencies on the other.

> You know that the consequences of the decision to be reached are likely to have a very heavy impact one way or another, and the decision has to be reached on what is often very ambiguous evidence.

Some of these ambiguous situations will be explored in the two case studies below.

Julie, aged 10: how long should she stay in mainstream school?
One of the heads quoted Julie as an instance of a situation in which he was involved at the time. She was ten, had Down's Syndrome, and had been apparently successfully integrated into school since she was five. Her parents and the support agencies were keen that Julie should stay in mainstream school as long as possible, quoting the perfectly valid, usual arguments about neighbourhood school, access to a broad curriculum, learning to establish links with non-disabled friends, keeping her school friends and her home friends the same, and participating in the full range of situations including sports days, school trips, and out of school activities based round the school. The LEA had been supportive, and Julie had a half-time classroom assistant who worked well with the class teacher, Julie herself, and indeed with the

specialist support agencies. On the other hand, the head and the class teacher saw Julie's friendships becoming more and more one-sided over the years, until now almost all the approaches were made by Julie. She was becoming increasingly isolated as her friends from earlier years developed social relationships and patterns of play that were far too complex for her to take meaningful part in, except as a happily tolerated 'class mascot'.

Was this the best kind of social environment for Julie to develop friendships? Julie's classmates were a fairly able group, and her class teacher was expecting a good performance at the Key Stage 2 tests. Julie was still working towards Level 1 on most of the academic targets, and although the classroom assistant was usefully occupying her during lessons, the class teacher was becoming increasingly concerned that the material in the National Curriculum seemed more and more removed from Julie's real curricular needs. She, and the head, were perfectly well aware that the National Curriculum had been drawn up with very little attention to the needs of children with disabilities. They saw much of the time that Julie was in class as being wasted in the sense that the material being covered was of very dubious relevance to her and she was missing out on experiences of mastery learning based on much more concrete situations than her classmates either needed or had time for.

The class teacher, and the head, were increasingly coming to the view that this curriculum could not possibly be the best the education system had to offer to Julie, and could not be said to be meeting her needs without a very wide stretch of the imagination. At the next annual review they had decided to raise the issue very seriously with the parents and support staff that Julie's needs were no longer being met in the school on both intellectual and social grounds, and to insist that the parents and the educational psychologist, in particular, very seriously considered what benefits would accrue to Julie if she did move to the nearby special school for children with moderate learning difficulties. At this point the head had no intention of forcing the issue of Julie moving to alternative provision, but he felt with increasing strength that to let the current situation continue unchallenged was an opting out of his responsibility to Julie.

Wayne, aged fourteen: was fighting becoming his way of life?

Wayne was fourteen, an anxious, active, and very quick-tempered lad, who had lived with his dad for the last four years. Wayne's basic skills in school were poor for his age, but not as poor as some of the other children in his year group, and by themselves not so poor as to imply he could not take part appropriately in the lessons. However, Wayne's interest in most of the subjects of the National Curriculum was pretty much zero, and there were only a few teachers in school who succeeded in involving him usefully in lessons, at least to judge by the criteria that Wayne produced some meaningful written work and avoided getting into trouble through arguing and fighting with other children. These teachers tended to be ones who knew

Wayne well from his earlier years in school, were experienced in teaching the subjects and were able to anticipate the kind of difficulties Wayne had in completing the tasks. They also were sufficiently in control of the class in general to give Wayne sufficient attention to keep his mind somewhere near the lesson content rather than irritating his neighbours. However, there were only a few teachers in school with this mix of skills, and so in many lessons Wayne appeared to achieve nothing but minor or major disruption.

The school had tried to enrol Wayne's father, but Wayne was the apple of his father's eye and in this instance parental involvement appeared to have made no difference to Wayne's behaviour. Wayne was at Stage 3 of the Code Of Practice, and the specialist behaviour support services and the educational psychology service had been involved. This had improved things slightly, in that now more of Wayne's subject teachers understood something of his difficulties and of possible ways to encourage his participation in lessons. Outside the classroom however his behaviour seemed to be deteriorating, and he seemed to be associated with most of the minor and major instances of verbal aggression occurring in the playground, and occasionally his play fighting turned serious. He had gained a reputation as a fighter in school, and appeared to be accepting this.

For the time being, Wayne was containable in school, but the school special needs coordinator and the head felt very strongly that Wayne was not receiving the kind of education which actually met his needs. They accepted the view of the educational psychologist and the behaviour support teacher that usually children who attended the authority's schools for children with emotional and behaviour disorders had considerably greater difficulties than Wayne did, in general showing greater difficulty in forming and maintaining relationships, and had poorer levels of basic skills of reading, writing and number. However, was a mainstream comprehensive school the best that the community could offer Wayne? The core of the head's dilemma seemed to be that while the school was managing Wayne's behaviour in school most of the time, the head saw Wayne as learning that he could be moderately aggressive with many other children and some of the teachers for a fair proportion of the time, as long as he stayed within certain boundaries. What would happen when he left school at 16 and began looking for work? There would be far fewer people around then to manage his behaviour and draw the firm boundaries for him. It seemed likely that he would gain no examination passes, and the head saw the school and indeed the entire education system as failing Wayne in a pretty disastrous way. In addition of course the constant emotional interaction with Wayne was wearing on the energies of his staff, and two parents of other boys had complained this term about Wayne fighting with their sons on the way home from school.

The head felt the need actively to manage the situation involving Wayne, rather than let things drift, and at present the only way of doing this seemed to be to work towards persuading the support services that Wayne really did need a place in a special unit, even though he could see all the disadvantages for Wayne in this outcome, as well as some of the advantages. If such a unit achieved a degree of change in Wayne's attainment and behaviour, it would be possible Wayne would leave school at 16, hopefully more in control of his behaviour, with better basic skills, and with the benefits of having developed some positive relationships with authority figures. On the debit side, the head accepted that Wayne would be leaving school with an idea of himself as being different, and with his local reputation made for getting into trouble made worse by leaving school from a special school.

This was, of course, always assuming that the local schools for emotionally disturbed children would accept lads as old as fourteen, or that the LEA had set up its Pupil Referral Unit by the time Wayne needed it. If events caught up with school and Wayne, and he did get into another serious fight, or was physically aggressive to a teacher, the exclusion road out of school early was certainly equally possible, and possibly more likely. The failure of all concerned to give Wayne a decent education would be even more apparent.

In these two case studies, the heads felt their schools were failing to educate the two children effectively, and their judgement was tending to the view that the children would be better off elsewhere. This was based on the children's lack of progress, the Heads' values of acting in what they considered the child's best interests, and of recognising the limits of their competence to manage their schools in a way that would deliver effective education for these children. They, and their schools, had tried hard, but saw themselves as clearly failing to achieve progress. In many ways, the easiest option was to let events take their course, and let relationships and communication patterns fragment to the point that the children concerned felt rejected, alienated and in their different ways, withdraw from school life through absence. Was this the best way for the situations to develop? They felt not, but were aware that in challenging the placement they would be seen as rejecting the children concerned.

Clearly, such dilemmas are familiar to many parents and professionals associated with children who have some degree of special need. Their familiarity does not however guarantee their resolution. Greater resourcing and staff training would help to some extent, but the underlying issue of the appropriateness of the National Curriculum as taught in mainstream schools for children with special needs remains. Is this the best we can offer Julie and Wayne?

Chapter 6

Assessment and Patterns of Educational Provision

Derrick Armstrong

Children with emotional and behavioural difficulties are the focus of considerable attention in school, often because they disturb the established norms of behaviour expected of children and therefore challenge the basis of adult leadership. This can raise the anxiety levels of teachers, who even without these concerns have a challenging and demanding role, and can influence the operation of systems of identification and provision of effective education for these children. This chapter will draw on research carried out by the author and his colleagues into the procedures for assessing and statementing children with special educational needs to consider some of the ways in which children may come to be identified as having emotional and behavioural difficulties, and the decision-making processes leading to provision being made for them (Armstrong 1995; Galloway *et al.* 1994). The values inherent in the provision and decision making process will be explored in the context of dilemmas that frequently occur in this area which include, for instance, apparent conflicts between providing effective education for the child experiencing difficulties and providing effective education for the rest of the children in the group; the extent to which the primary accountability of the school should be towards achieving as high examination successes as possible for the children with no special needs at the expense of the progress of children with statements of special educational needs; and the tendency for the provision of unit-based education for children with emotional and behavioural problems to increase the proportion of students who are thought to need such provision.

The problem of identification: what are emotional and behavioural difficulties?

Concerns about the misbehaviour of young people are nothing new and are rarely far from the news headlines. In the last century riots by public school pupils were quelled by the army (Gathorne-Hardy 1977). Prior to compulsory education the Poor Law was used to transport troublesome children from the lower classes to the colonies. Workhouse and 'ragged' schools were also established to control those seen as a danger to society (Hurt 1988). More recently the headlines of our popular press have been grabbed by disturbing stories of the mayhem wreaked by pupils at The Ridings school in West Yorkshire. The truth behind these headlines, if ever told, is likely to be far more complex than that suggested by the soundbites and camera images of politicians, union leaders and media-makers. However, the politics that underpin these events are never far from the surface and the different interpretations placed on the personal and social tragedies that sometimes so publicly unfold rest upon value positions that are highly significant in their own right.

It is important that concerns about the behaviour of young people at any given time are seen within their proper social and historical context. Understanding the complexity of the issues is not helped, for instance, by simplistically equating the behaviour of public school boys in the 18th century with alienated and disaffected working class youth of late 20th century Britain. Similarly, the experience of teachers and their role in society is very different in the late 20th century compared with the 18th century, and these differences are likely to have very different outcomes in relation both to an understanding of children's difficulties and for the management of their behaviour.

The concept of 'emotional and behavioural' difficulties is itself far from a neutral description of behaviour that fits neatly into some psychological category. Yet the concept is frequently used in this way, encouraging the pathologising of problem behaviour in schools in terms of personal deficits. By placing such a construction on children's behaviour attention is moved away from a wider consideration of the social processes of schooling and the effects of changes in the function and role of schooling in our own time. This is not to argue against the value of psychology *per se* but it is to argue for an examination of psychological categories and processes as located in and by historical and cultural contexts (Cole 1977).

The Warnock Report (DES 1978) and the legislation that followed provide very good examples of how the effects of social change have been individualised through the language and procedures of 'special' education systems. Increases in provision for special educational needs have inevitably led, it seems, to larger numbers of children being identified as having needs which then, interestingly, becomes a justification for the original decision to expand provision. The circularity of this justification is used to avoid consideration, for instance, of those changes in society that have led to widespread unemployment and unemployability for young people who do not achieve examination successes at school (Galloway *et al.* 1994; Tomlinson 1988). Of course the Warnock Report is famous for its abandonment of the medical model and its emphasis upon educational need and the contexts within which those needs arise. Despite its ideological break with the view that educational provision must be defined in terms of functional impairment (i.e. the assumption that a child who is visually impaired, for instance, would necessarily benefit from a particular form of education 'treatment') the Warnock Report advanced a theory of 'needs' which individualised experiences as, for instance, 'emotional and behavioural disorders' which were represented as the product of 'difficult home circumstances, adverse temperamental characteristics and brain dysfunction'. (para. 11.60)

The disingenuity of Warnock's description of emotional and behavioural difficulties is matched only by the oppressiveness of the conclusions that were drawn from it. It is disingenuous in that it substitutes broad value-based descriptions of behaviour for serious critical analysis of the conditions under which those behaviours occur. This leads to the conclusion that our primary concern should be with addressing the within child symptoms or outcomes of social dysfunctions rather than understanding and challenging the social disadvantage and oppression that lie under the surface of social education, emotional dislocation and educational failure. This value position in relation to the social conditions of disabling identities is something that goes to the heart of the Warnock Report and its discourse of needs.

In stark contrast to Warnock's assumptions and values Galloway and Goodwin (1987) have argued that a term like 'maladjustment' or 'emotional and behavioural difficulties' 'is at best a ragbag term for describing any type of behaviour which teachers, psychologists or doctors find disturbing'. (p.32)

The difference between these viewpoints emanates from very different value perspectives. Significantly, while Warnock recognises that problems with learning and behaviour occur in a social context, the value position that informs strategies of intervention is one that emphasises the individual character of that response, be it the individual child, individual teacher, individual classroom, or individual school. The critique advanced by Galloway and Goodwin, by contrast, raises issues about the character of professionalism itself and the political choices that inform educational policies and educational opportunities.

Professional values and the assessment of emotional and behavioural difficulties

Prevailing models of assessment may be heavily influenced by genuine concerns about the importance of identifying the needs of the 'whole child', yet in practice these procedures may actually focus upon negotiations over areas of professional responsibility and authority in the context of decision-making about the management of resources. This can be seen, for instance, in the area of parent–professional cooperation during assessment procedures. From the perspective of professionals, where parents broadly accept their guidance and, more importantly, accept the authority of their expert judgement, partnership might be built upon a reasonably firm footing. From the perspective of parents, insofar as the assessment takes place within the parameters of an established professional culture which has established the 'rules of engagement' between participants, the procedures may appear bureaucratic, with the consequence that their own contribution is rendered ineffective.

One of the consequences of professional cultures is that they lead to rivalry between professions. Where a child is perceived to have different, possibly conflicting needs, and these are identified as lying principally within the area of interest of more than one professional group the multi-disciplinary process may become a forum for the negotiation of professional identities and roles. When the outcome of an assessment is constrained by the availability of resources the scope for interdisciplinary collaboration may be further reduced, leading to new conflicts over professional identities.

For instance, where a particular agency clearly has responsibility for a client or where responsibility is clearly rejected by one or more groups of professionals (as is the case where a child is permanently excluded from school) assessment may be largely a bureaucratic exercise. For this reason multi-disciplinary assessment may be seen as irrelevant by professionals and parents alike, despite the fact that their contributions have been officially sought. Parents in particular may be disempowered by the cultural milieu in which assessments occur. As one parent put it when interviewed: 'The educational psychologist says if I challenge any of the reports the kids can't go to the school, so I don't really have a say. I've got to take everything they say'.

The desire to get their child back into school, at almost any cost, is a powerful consideration for parents.

The status of parental contributions is undermined by this combination of powerlessness (to contest professional decisions) and vulnerability (having to cope with the consequences of professional inaction as well as professional actions). Moreover, parents can also be cast in the role of members of a second-tier 'team', being excluded from discussions concerned with the allocation of resources. The validity of a distinction between identification and resourcing of needs is a tenuous one. In the absence of clear-cut clinical criteria the availability of resources has inevitable consequences for what 'needs' are identified and the ways in which those 'needs' are understood in the assessment. By being excluded from these former discussions parents are excluded from participation in decision making about the framework within which their children's needs will subsequently be identified and addressed.

Where responsibility for meeting the child's needs, including both professional and financial responsibility, is unclear or contested the assessment procedures may then become a forum for negotiations between professionals about the authority and responsibilities of their respective agencies. While the outcome of these negotiations is usually concerned with the ownership and control of resources, the negotiations themselves are more likely to focus upon the professional role and authority of the different participants; in other words, upon ownership of the client. These negotiations illustrate what Fulcher (1989) has referred to as 'fragmented professionalism'. While explicit professional rivalry is replaced by a service ideal of shared responsibility for the 'whole child', negotiations between professionals over whether to accept or reject a client become considerably more important. This is apparent, for instance, in the following case study of negotiations between education and social services personnel.

The role of social workers varies from case to case but where they are providing family support social workers may come into conflict with professionals from other agencies. Robin's social worker, for example, saw her role as being 'to filter and translate' the assessment being carried out by the LEA because there is a lot of 'verbal nodding and winking' as different professionals: 'try to persuade parents they are working in their best interests whilst covering up the lack of provision – making the best of a bad situation in the face of a lot of personal trauma'.

Following Robin's permanent exclusion from school for aggressive behaviour towards his teachers the local authority had to decide whether or not to initiate statutory assessment procedures. While the education authority was considering its actions Robin, who was 15, was temporarily taken into the care of the local authority. The education authority called a case conference to which Robin's social worker was invited. Robin's teachers made it clear that they would not have him back in school. However, the educational psychologist was unwilling to recommend a special school placement because he believed Robin's academic needs could not be properly met within a special school. A senior social worker expressed concern about the family situation and identified the importance of removing him from this 'disturbed' environment as the main priority. Yet he also had doubts about the ability of his department to act effectively in this case because 'our evidence might not stand up in a court'. He tried, therefore, to persuade the education authority that Robin's needs would best be served by a placement in a residential special school made under a statement of special educational needs. The negotiations between psychologist and social worker focused on two questions: first, that of which agency had the principal responsibility for Robin; second, how, and by whom, resources could be released to meet the needs that had been identified in answer to the first question. In consequence, this assessment was characterised by the attempts by different agencies to negotiate a consensus based upon their own assessment of priorities and available resources.

The education authority was seen by the social services department as having the authority to act (under the statementing procedures) and having access to resources that could be made available to meet Robin's needs. Therefore Robin's social workers attempted to negotiate a definition of Robin's special educational needs in terms of his social and emotional interests. To this end they obtained their own psychologist's report from a social services unit which argued that Robin's educational needs could not be met unless his emotional needs were first dealt with by removing him from his family home. This suggestion was rejected outright by the educational psychologist who, at the outset, conceptualised Robin's interests in terms of his educational needs alone. Moreover, the educational psychologist believed his own professional integrity was being attacked which reinforced his refusal, as the LEA's representative in the negotiations with the social services department, to commit the LEA resources to the very different priorities of the social services department.

Contested notions of professionalism, marketisation, competition and deprofessionalisation

The social and political context in which special educational services are today provided is very different from that which existed in the late 1970s when the philosophy underpinning the organisation of provision was developed in the Warnock Report. In the late 1990s the contraction of opportunities for young people together with the marketisation of education has fuelled the competition between schools. Moreover, the ability of schools to defuse dissent is threatened by economic changes that have left large numbers of young people excluded to the margins of our society. Increasingly there are children who perceive education as a poor investment and who see no benefits to be gained from conforming to the values the system promotes. The continuing trend for schools physically to exclude these children is a reminder of the pressures in our society which create conditions of social alienation and also of the difficulties faced by educational professionals whose roles have been radically restructured by government policies over the last two decades.

Professionals working with children who are presenting difficult behaviours may be sensitive to the wider social and political contexts within which those behaviours occur but nonetheless may feel constrained by the circumstances of their own working lives to respond in particular ways. When a child is referred for assessment it is unlikely to be the result solely of a disinterested concern to identify a child's special educational needs. The expectations teachers have of the assessment outcome, including concerns over the acquisition of resources or the removal of a troublesome child, are all factors which are likely to bear upon the decision making process. For these reasons educational professionals do not and *cannot* assess a child's needs without also taking into account and responding to the legitimate expectations of other participants with interests in the outcome of particular assessments. Psychologists, for instance, may feel constrained to negotiate solutions which are acceptable to the schools for whom they are advisers, to their LEA employers and to the parents of children who are the subject of assessment. These constraints reflect some of the deeper ambiguities about the relationship between professionals as both service providers and members of the state's administrative bureaucracy on the one hand and service users on the other hand.

Educational professionals play a crucial role in modern societies. The origins of this role are fairly recent and in Britain can be located in the post-war policies of the welfare state. These policies, of which special education is one example, might be seen as reflecting the humanitarian concerns of social reformers immediately following a protracted period of war. However, the expansion of these services has been accompanied by *bureaucratised* practices which Fulcher (1989) has referred to as an 'entrenched professionalism'. These practices refer not simply to the promotion by professionals of their own interests but rather to the relationship between professionals and the state. While the state acts as mediator between the different professions and their clients defining who those clients should be and how they should be helped, the state is itself also the client because professional agencies exist to deliver services which are provided by the state.

A consequence of recent government policies, and indeed perhaps also one of its purposes, has been the undermining of the homogeneity of professional interests through the marketisation of professional services. In these circumstances professionals are increasingly involved in negotiations over the scope of their own expertise and the 'needs' of their clients. The professional practice of educational psychologists provides a good example of how these processes work.

Advice from the Department for Education and Employment makes it clear that assessments should be carried out without regard to the type of provision available within the LEA. However, where competition for scarce resources is intense psychologists, whose contribution to special educational assessment is pivotal, may encounter pressures that make it difficult to avoid considering the availability and distribution of resources. This can operate entirely at an informal level as is the case when psychologists perceive their professional credibility with schools and parents to be dependent upon recommendations which can realistically be delivered. At a more formal level educational psychologists may be drawn directly into the decision making process where they are called upon in their role as LEA officers, as distinct from professional advisers, to provide the LEA with advice on the placement and resource implications of different options. The consequent ethical and professional dilemmas (Lindsay 1996) can seriously affect the ability of psychologists to represent the interests of any or all of their clients resulting in reactive practices rather than proactive interventions. To some extent these tensions and consequent ethical dilemmas about who their clients are have always been implicit where the psychologists have been the gate keepers to resources. In practice these tensions have largely been resolved through the development of a consensus model of decision making. Thus in situations of conflict between the competing interests of different clients psychologists have tended to understand their role in terms of the resolution of conflict through the negotiation of a consensus. A compromise is aimed for whereby different participants will see their own needs being met through decisions taken in respect of the child's special educational needs.

However, the consensus model is particularly poor at handling questions relating to the differential distribution of power between participants. It fails to address the issue of how power is conveyed and perpetuated through the assessment procedures. For instance, conflict with powerful interest groups can threaten the professional autonomy and therefore the professional interests of psychologists. Yet the form of control to which psychologists, as members of the state bureaucracy, are subject (i.e. the mediation of the state between professionals and service users to define client needs) not only means that it can be unclear who their clients are but also that they are placed into positions where their actions and decisions necessarily come into conflict with the interests of those whom psychologists would define as their principal clients, e.g. children. This conflict is embedded structurally in psychologists' role through the power of the state to specify and define the needs of service users. This relationship to the state is not necessarily reproduced in the subjective understanding of professionals in their day to day practice. From this perspective the service user (e.g. the child) is invariably seen as the principal or even sole client. Regardless of the humanitarian principles which psychologists adopt when viewing their own actions, this subjective understanding of who the clients are can itself serve to veil the range of conflicting interests which influence their practice in ways which operate to disempower not only the service users but the professionals as well.

In the changed political and economic climate of the 1980s and 1990s, characterised by the assertion of an ideology of individual responsibility for individual need and a policy of public expenditure reduction (see Chapter 2), professional assessment of children's needs can no longer be adequately understood solely in terms of the application of specialised systems of knowledge. This has had a considerable effect on the role of professionals carrying out assessments.

As the relationship between the state and service users has been reconstructed under the influence of neo-liberalism there has been a growing fragmentation of professional roles and responsibilities with different occupational groups competing for ownership of clients. The introduction of a national curriculum to be followed in all state schools has removed from teachers the control they once had over what is taught in schools. The procedures for nationally assessing the learning of all children at 'key stages' of their schooling, together with the publication of each school's results, has forced teachers to be accountable for the delivery of a curriculum over which they may perceive themselves to have little control. In addition, these procedures have created conditions of work intensification which contribute further to the deskilling process. In consequence of these changes in their professional responsibilities the deskilling of teachers may take place at two levels. In the first place, the professional status of teachers is undermined by the loss of skill and autonomy, the increase of stress, the increase of supervision and the creation of a new managerial bureaucracy within schools whose concerns rest primarily with competitiveness and budgetary control. Secondly, the loss of professional autonomy and control which teachers feel themselves to have suffered may lead to responsibility for 'problem' children being shifted into the hands of outside 'experts', including educational psychologists and the staff of specialist schools. The apparent willingness of teachers to identify large numbers of children whose needs cannot be met in their mainstream schools might be understood as reflecting this process of deskilling. The appeal to outside 'experts', such as psychologists, may indicate a narrowing of the skills to which teachers are able to lay claim. Where schools are under pressure to adopt pupil selection and financial policies that maximise their competitiveness in the market-place, classroom teachers may respond to pressures from their own management teams by refusing to accept responsibility for severely disruptive pupils with the consequence that teaching is routinised in terms of the administration of the 'normal' curriculum for 'normal' children.

It may be misleading, however, to understand these trends simply in terms of a 'deskilling' thesis. Teachers may actually resist attempts to deskill their work by negotiating their role as 'skilful' in the day to day work relations of their school. Such strategies are not without their contradictions but an exploration of these contradictions may provide some useful insights into professional values and identities. Observations made of meetings between teachers and psychologists during my own research on the assessment of emotional and behavioural difficulties suggested how reskilling strategies may operate.

The educational report that a school provides for the LEA constitutes the formal part of its contribution to the assessment while an informal part is frequently found in teachers' negotiations with educational psychologists and their LEAs regarding the nature of the 'problem' and how it should be dealt with. When teachers identify children as having emotional and behavioural difficulties they frequently believe the behaviour of these children to be qualitatively different from the behaviour of 'ordinary' children. Describing a child with 'emotional problems' one teacher stated 'I've got a very bad class this year. A lot of difficult boys. But Damien isn't like them. With them it's because they get no discipline. With Damien that's not it. He's just strange'. In labelling behaviour as disturbed rather than disruptive an implicit claim is made about the irrationality of that behaviour and therefore that a child suffering from an *emotional* disturbance needs specialist treatment that cannot be provided by a mainstream school. The supposed irrationality of the behaviour legitimises the removal of the child into special education but it also legitimises the school's failure to effect changes in the child's behaviour. Where teachers believe that a child cannot exercise rational control over behaviour it is assumed that they cannot be held responsible for that child's behaviour in the classroom. In other words, when teachers requested an assessment of a child who they claimed had emotional and behavioural difficulties, implicit in this request was a parallel claim that the child's unacceptable behaviour was not influenced by practices within the classroom or school.

By contrast teachers identified children as disruptive rather than disturbed where they believed they could manage with the resources ordinarily available to them in their schools. Where it was felt that children's behaviour demanded the allocation of resources and facilities not normally available within mainstream schools they were then likely to be identified as having 'emotional problems'. This emphasis upon resources reflects very accurately the criteria adopted by the 1981 Education Act to define special educational needs.

The decision to refer a child for assessment does not imply a perception on the part of teachers making the referral that they lack appropriate skills. Indeed the decision by an LEA to initiate an assessment may reflect the success of teacher negotiations as they seek to define their role in terms of their skills with more able, higher status, children. Once a decision has been taken to refer a child for assessment, this decision will be a major factor affecting future developments. Henceforward, those who are involved in the formal assessment must take account of the needs of those who are disturbed by the child's behaviour, difficulties with learning, or physical or sensory disabilities. Moreover, the decision to refer a child for assessment is usually made in anticipation of a particular outcome; either the removal of a child from the school or the acquisition of additional resources. In consequence the statementing procedures are often seen by teachers as a bureaucratic mechanism for effecting that outcome. As one head teacher argued:

> I felt we had our quota of disturbed children ... It was a shame he had to go home where the problems were but there was a lot of disruption in the class and other children would be affected. The class was a different place after he had gone ... The fact that he has been removed from school is a plus for us, the other children and the staff. We hate excluding children but our hands are tied.

Such views resulted in quite specific expectations about the outcome of the assessment, often that the child would not return to the school. Educational psychologists were generally very sympathetic to the position teachers were in but also recognised that certain actions taken by teachers such as permanent exclusions 'shut doors in terms of possible recommendations'.

Senior staff at David's school were confident that they had the skills and resources to meet his needs. However, David's parents were concerned about his behaviour and persuaded them to seek a psychologist's opinion. It later emerged that David had been referred to the school psychological service when at primary school and had been described on this occasion by his head teacher as 'a very disturbed child'. At this point David's teachers put pressure on the educational psychologist and the LEA to initiate a formal assessment of his special educational needs with a view to a formal statement of those needs being issued. In response to this request the psychologist and staff from the behavioural support service entered into discussions with David's teachers, and eventually agreed to recommend a formal assessment under the Act. Although

David's statement of special educational needs, when issued, did no more than formally endorse the existing arrangements, the school, nonetheless, saw this as a legal document which would in some unspecified way impose an obligation on the LEA to make alternative arrangements for David if his behaviour were to deteriorate. From the perspective of David's teachers, far from resulting in a transfer of their skills to the psychologist the assessment had concluded with a successful negotiation of their own needs that gave recognition to the skills embedded in their professional role. Whilst the management of classroom behaviour was seen as comprising one of those skills, dealing with the 'disturbed' child whose behaviour, because of its irrationality, posed particular difficulties in the context of an ordinary classroom was not seen as falling within the professional responsibilities of these teachers. David's teachers believed that in a one-to-one or small group setting they could effectively meet the educational needs of a disturbed child. However, for them this was not the issue because (a) the education of the disturbed child could not be managed effectively within the context and resources of the ordinary classroom; (b) the presence of a disturbed child in the ordinary classroom seriously impeded the learning of all children in that classroom; and, (c) their skills were principally related to the 'higher status' concerns of educating 'ordinary' children rather than to teaching children with special needs. By insisting on alternative provision for David if his behaviour was to deteriorate, his teachers were legitimising their perception of their professional role.

Conclusion

The power of educational professionals is derived from their administrative role within the bureaucracy of the state, not simply from their professional expertise. Ultimately it is the state that defines clients' needs and how these needs are to be met. Therefore, the interests of professional groups are tied up not only with the state but *with the relationship between the state and client groups*. Because the state incorporates different interests, professionals are less constrained by common professional values than would be the case if client needs were defined by the professional agencies themselves. However, as government policy has led to professionals increasingly playing an explicitly administrative role (whether that be in the form of educational psychologists servicing statements of special educational needs or of teachers administering a national curriculum) the contradictions between professional services performed on behalf of clients and bureaucratic functions performed on behalf of the state have been more sharply defined. On the one hand, these constraints limit the freedom of professional agencies to define the parameters of their own activities while, on the other, they lead to a more fragmented perception of professional interest linked to concerns from within these occupational groups over the deskilling of their work. This has the consequence of bringing professionals into conflict with each other as they attempt to negotiate a new consensus about their respective professional roles, the value systems which guide their beliefs and actions and, by implication, a consensus about the needs of particular children.

Government policy, far from valuing schools which are successful with children with social, emotional and behavioural difficulties, actually focuses attention on the achievements of more able children. For this reason more pupils are being identified as having special educational needs. Although this may be understood as reflecting the deprofessionalisation of teachers an alternative interpretation suggests how teachers may employ strategies which enhance the status of their professional role through an emphasis upon teaching skills with academically able and motivated children.

The identification of a child as having special educational needs may ensure that the professional competence of those with responsibility for that child in the mainstream schools is not brought into question. In particular, where a child is identified as 'emotionally disturbed' teachers may view this as less threatening to perceptions of their competence as teachers than might be the case had the child merely been labelled disruptive. While the latter might raise questions about the teacher's classroom management skills, the former assumes that the child's personality and emotional or family history make it difficult for him or her to respond rationally in 'normal' classroom situations.

Far from undermining the professional responsibilities of teachers, the assessment procedures may actually provide mainstream teachers with the opportunity to enter into negotiations with other educational professionals about the nature of their teaching role, resulting in a re-definition of their expertise in terms of higher status skills associated with teaching more able children. The removal of disturbed children is legitimised in terms of this conceptualisation of the teachers' role, and consequently allows teachers to evaluate positively their role and competence. In turn this child-centred focus can constrain the type of intervention available to educational psychologists forcing them to respond to the way teachers initially define the problem.

Teachers may ask for children to be seen by psychologists in order to establish or negotiate a particular definition of their own professional skill as teachers. These teachers see themselves making a crucial contribution to the identification of children's special educational needs while psychologists and other outside experts may be seen primarily as gate keepers to resources. Where this is so, the recommendations made by these 'experts' will be influenced by the strategies adopted by teachers. At one level this may be seen as evidence of teachers being deskilled since outside 'experts' increasingly become responsible for an area of work previously under the control of teachers (the identification of the needs of disturbing children and the planning of specialist programmes for their children). However, evidence has been presented in this chapter which suggests teachers may counter measures that tend to deprofessionalise their role by adopting strategies aimed at re-negotiating their role with 'ordinary' children as 'skilful'. The referral to outside experts of children who present difficult or disturbing behaviour in the classroom may constitute just such a strategy. Where a statement of special educational needs is provided this is likely to be seen by teachers, not as evidence of a lack of skill on their part, but as the outcome of a successful negotiation of those professional skills.

Acknowledgements

The research on which this chapter is based was funded by the Economic and Social Research Council (Grant no. R 000 23 1393) and was directed by Professor David Galloway and Professor Sally Tomlinson. The support of the Research Council and of the Project Directors is gratefully acknowledged.

Chapter 7

The Establishment of Whole School Policies

Sonia Sharp and David Thompson

> All human life and all human civilisation is about values.
> DeBono 1985 (p.63).

What is a whole school policy?

A whole school policy is a document which describes the aims of the school in relation to a particular aspect of curriculum management or school organisation. Most policies also state how the school will achieve these aims and how they will evaluate their progress in meeting them. A whole school policy is one which all members of the school community are expected to know and implement. Ideally, the preparation of the policy is also achieved through community involvement. Other policies may only relate to specific sections of the school community. The whole school policy becomes a set of guidelines which are expected to shape the behaviour and actions of staff and students.

The types of issues addressed by whole school policies are usually those which govern fundamental aspects of school life deemed important for the delivery of effective education. They reflect the values of society and the school regarding the essential ingredients of 'good' educational practice and therefore provide some first principles which underpin day to day life in the school. In essence, the existence of school policies aims to establish consistency of practice throughout the school and therefore they often relate to social and pastoral aspects of school life such as equal opportunities, behaviour management, bullying or to aspects of curriculum delivery which are integral to all subject areas such as the education of children with special educational needs. They implicitly communicate the key values of the school because they send the message, 'This is so important that *everybody* in the school will be influenced by it'.

Values arise from beliefs. From beliefs and values we go on to develop principles. The purpose of values, beliefs and principles is to enable us to organise and make sense of the world around us and to make decisions expediently (DeBono 1985). Once we have beliefs, values and principles we can develop guidelines for shaping our own behaviour and for interpreting the behaviour of others. Whole school policies are publicly stated organisational guidelines based on mutually accepted beliefs, values and principles. When they are properly implemented they communicate and reinforce those values in the way they affect practice. They provide a framework against which staff and students can judge the appropriateness of their actions and decisions. Indeed without the framework of a policy then classroom practice in a school could become diverse and idiosyncratic, reflecting the individual values of the teachers rather than the organisational values of the school. The power of values to influence practice should not be underestimated. As Kohn (1986) writes:

> Teachers'... choice of stories, the order in which they are taught, and the tone of voice in which the character is mentioned; the fact the children must raise their hands to speak or obtain permission to go to the bathroom or address one person in the room by his or her last name; the objects that decorate the walls and who decided they should be there; how students' work is evaluated (and for what purpose) – all of these and many other aspects of life at school already vibrate with values whether we realise it or not. There is no question of introducing values into a neutral environment, but only of critically examining existing values in light of others which could be there instead. (p.198.)

The convergence of different sets of values

The primary values of a school will be related to learning. However, in the day to day delivery of the curriculum schools take into account the values of a range of people who are part of the wider school community. Within this wider school community there will be different groups. Parents, as well as being concerned with learning, are likely to have values about their child being cared for and being safe. Students themselves may have values about being accepted by peers and belonging. Different teachers will have different beliefs and values about education. Watts (1989) identifies four key groups who are powerful influences on the way in which a school delivers its curriculum. These are:
- parents and neighbours
- local power holders (governors, local and national government, voluntary groups)
- the teaching profession
- the media.

Each of these groups may push for particular values, some of which may be in conflict with those upheld by the senior managers in the school. These conflicts may lead to the design of solutions which can relate to the different sets of values or alternatively may lead to discord and difficulty. The extent to which any one group is able to influence practice within the school will depend upon how strong and how widespread the beliefs and values of the group are. Values which are imposed upon the senior management and teachers within the school may be fully embraced or may be accepted on the surface as a way of managing relationships with that group without actually influencing practice within the classroom or playgrounds. This latter route is likely to lead to disappointment and disaffection once the group who have pushed for the values realise that their acceptance has been tokenistic. Whole school policies enable schools to achieve consensus about educational values and cooperation in a meaningful way and reduce the likelihood of dissension and dissatisfaction. The process of policy development which includes discussion, operational definitions and review, can lead to the establishment of integrated procedures which relate to varied value systems.

One of the important motivators for being part of a group or organisation is belief confirmation (Tyson and Jackson 1992). Membership of groups who express values contributes to a sense of identity. Through belonging to a group or organisation which shares similar values individuals are assured that their beliefs and values are reasonable and accurate. Whilst parents were restricted to sending their child to the most local school or paying for private education, the extent of belief confirmation provided by the school varied from community to community. Recent government legislation which has led to increased parental choice over school and greater opportunities for schools to specialise may lead to more strongly stated educational values in schools.

Financial viability for schools depends on student numbers. How do schools attract students? By convincing parents that they offer the best geographically accessible education for their child. How do we make judgements about what constitutes 'good' education? By comparing what is on offer against our own beliefs, values and principles about education. How does a head teacher market the school? By promoting values which are important to parents. Thus values have become a commodity. This is fine if the values being promoted and reinforced are positive. Unfortunately, just as belief confirmation can lead to affirmation of positive values, it can also lead to reinforcement of values which are based on mistaken beliefs or stereotyped views. A recent example of this has emerged in Bradford where parents of white children have chosen to place their children in schools in a neighbouring authority which have few black families. The local community schools are consequently educating mainly Asian children. In this case the practice of a group of parents is leading to the maintenance of racially segregated education. Similar pressures can be placed on head teachers to accept segregation of children with special educational needs, especially if parents and teachers believe that meeting the needs of some children leads to deprivation of others.

The central role of senior management

The values and beliefs which prevail within a school community will influence the content of the policy and the way in which it is developed. The senior managers and governors of the school will directly and indirectly influence this. Firstly, they set the overall aims of the school. These will be based on their own personal belief system and those values introduced by the wider community that they are willing to accept. The psychological profile of the senior management team in terms of motivation and beliefs about locus of control and child development will influence how they manage the school, who they recruit and support, which areas of school life they invest in, and which policies they develop. However, the existence of a whole school policy by itself will not provide complete insight into the values prevailing within the school. The content of the policy, the way in which the policy has been developed and the extent to which the policy is implemented will give a more accurate notion of how important the issue addressed by the policy really is. To illustrate this let's consider the practice of two schools in developing a special needs policy. In 1994 the Department for Education produced the 'Code of Practice on the identification and assessment of special educational needs'. Schools are expected to have regard for this Code of Practice and in doing so develop a whole school policy in relation to meeting the needs of individual children and appoint a member of staff responsible for coordinating practice within the school. Compare the practice of these two schools:

- *School 1:* Policy written by Special Needs Coordinator, ratified by head and governors, circulated to all staff. Special Needs Co-ordinator is a full time classroom teacher with no additional salary points for responsibility. Implementing the Code of Practice was put on the agenda of a staff meeting. Only half of the staff attended.
- *School 2:* Policy developed after extensive consultation with staff and series of staff training days on meeting the needs of children with special needs within the mainstream classroom. Every curriculum related policy is reviewed in respect of how the curriculum will be differentiated for children with special educational needs, including those who are very able. The special needs coordinator is a member of the senior management team and has 0.5 timetable protected to carry out this role. The head teacher agreed to forego an increase in personal salary to achieve this.

What does the practice of these two schools in relation to policy development and support for the special needs coordinator tell us about the values held by the school in relation to special educational needs? Both schools have a whole school policy on special needs and have appointed a special needs coordinator. However, how this has been achieved reflects a different set of values between the two schools, mostly resulting from the priority placed on the policy by the head teacher.

Values can be divided into two groups: higher values which are nonnegotiable and which we use to make major life decisions, and lower values which we can compromise in certain situations (DeBono 1985). The 'vision' created by the senior management which sets the ethos for the school will be based on higher values; the spectrum of values tolerated within the school will reflect lower values. What constitutes higher values and lower values will vary from school to school.

Conflicts of values are often managed in three ways. These are:
* by developing a hierarchy of values and agreeing that some are more important than others
* by mutually accepting the right for people to have different values
* by promoting discussion between those expressing different values and looking for areas of agreement on practice.

The extent to which a school can develop policies and practice based on values which are extremely different from those of the influential groups in the school community will depend on the ability of the senior management to persuade a significant proportion of people that the values proposed by the school are more important than those they hold themselves or that it is acceptable to have a different set of values operating within the school than in the community. John Watts (1992) talks about 'the Point'. The Point is the acceptable boundary within which divergence of values will be tolerated but beyond which they will not. Watts describes the role of head teacher as:

> mediator and interpreter, who stands at and advertises the boundary line between school and society, a Janus-like figure looking simultaneously inward to the institution and outward to the world around, guardian of the Point ... Quite literally, the survival of the institution, let alone its distinctive, innovative character will depend on this clear and steady recognition of the Point, up to which it may go, beyond which it may not.' (p.18)

The role of senior managers in the school, therefore, is not only to know their own beliefs, values and principles but also those of significant groups within the school and society at large. The maintenance of a successful and financially viable school will depend upon being able to establish the right environment for learning and to manage any value conflicts successfully. Establishing policies can assist in achieving this.

The influence of behaviour management

The establishment of whole school policies is relatively recent. The first tranche of 'whole school policies' arose as a result of the Report of the Elton Committee into Discipline in Schools (DES 1989). They recommended that schools develop whole school policies on behaviour management. Hitherto, most schools had a set of rules for student behaviour but the concept of policy goes far beyond 'rules'. A policy is a course of action – a strategic plan for achieving a stated aim. The Elton Committee defined the key elements of a 'good' whole school policy on behaviour. They recommended that whole school behaviour policies included:

- clear principles and rationale
- a minimal number of rules which are positively phrased
- a healthy balance between rewards and punishments
- fairness and consistency whilst allowing flexibility for individual circumstances
- an emphasis on collective responsibility for behaviour management
- no punishment of whole groups or individual humiliation
- clearly stated boundaries for on site and off site
- support for non-teaching staff
- direct action for bullying and harassment.

They also stated that the policy should be based on professional agreement arrived at through consultation and procedures should be established for regular monitoring and review. Subsequent research into behaviour management, in particular bullying, has enabled educationalists to understand more fully the dynamics and processes involved in the establishment of whole school policies which do influence the behaviour and attitudes of large chunks of the school community (Thompson and Sharp 1994). This work will be discussed in more detail later in this chapter. The Elton Committee emphasised the centrality of 'ethos' in promoting positive behaviour in schools. 'Ethos' is defined as the 'prevalent tone of sentiment of a people or community' (*The Shorter Oxford English Dictionary* 1983), in other words, a common set of values.

Developing policies as a way of shaping values

Between 1991 and 1993 a research team based in the Psychology Department at Sheffield University, directed by Peter Smith and funded by the Department for Education (DfE), investigated how schools could best tackle the problem of bullying behaviour (Smith and Sharp 1994). A key intervention implemented by all 23 schools involved in the project was to establish a whole school anti-bullying policy (Sharp and Thompson 1994). The project team noted that the schools which had developed their policies through an extensive process of discussion and debate with staff and students were most effective in reducing levels of bullying. Participation in the development process was time consuming; however it seemed that as a result of this involvement a shared view of bullying as 'not a good thing' was engendered. There was also understanding and agreement about how it was to be prevented and responded to. In a sense, the staff and students in these schools established a common value about bullying and from there went on to establish consistent practice in tackling it.

The example of the bullying policy is an interesting example of how school values and society values interact and develop. At the outset of the project, there was a small but significant group of parents who were protesting at the way their children had been bullied in school. This protest was picked up by the media who dwelled on the most extreme and negative outcomes of bullying in school. The government responded to the combined influence of media attention and parental pressure by funding the DfE Sheffield anti-bullying project and by putting pressure on schools through inspections to develop anti-bullying policies. At the outset of the project, the project team met with varied responses from schools. Although some teaching staff and parents believed that bullying was inappropriate behaviour and should be tackled, there were a significant group who justified inaction in the following ways:

- Bullying is a part of growing up. These kids have just got to toughen up and learn to stand up for themselves.
- I was bullied when I was at school and I am all right.
- It's only harmless fun. Some kids just can't take a joke.
- We are teachers not social workers. What has bullying got to do with education?
- Bullying is not a problem in our school so we don't need to do anything about it.
- If we do work on bullying, parents will think we have got a big problem.

However, by the end of the project there was a much more widely held view that bullying was widespread, was not acceptable and that 'good schools do something about bullying'. The outcomes of the project suggest that the process of policy development employed by these schools enabled an alignment of values amongst initially disparate groups. In the next section of this chapter we will consider the steps the schools took in order to achieve this.

The process of establishing a whole school policy

Effective school policies are those which are achieved through an extensive process of discussion and consultation and which are put into practice systematically and continuously. There are four stages of establishing a policy. These are:

- preparation: getting ready for the process
- development: setting up the policy
- implementation: ensuring it is used
- evaluation: reviewing its effectiveness.

Preparing for policy development
A planned approach to policy development will be more successful than a haphazard approach. Developing a policy which is going to shape values and behaviour requires the involvement of everybody in the school over a period

of time. This can be difficult to coordinate so good planning is essential.

The energy to begin and maintain policy development can be generated by a relatively small group of interested and motivated individuals. This working group could include representatives of the different groups (and therefore different sets of values) who come together within the school community such as staff, parents, governors and students. It should definitely include at least one member of senior management. The role of this group will be to plan and oversee the process of policy development and implementation. In doing this they will:

- make sure that the policy is on the agenda of key meetings over the next year
- facilitate and organise training events
- manage the consultation process
- draft the policy document
- set up the policy launch
- plan how the policy will be maintained, monitored and evaluated in the long term.

Because this working group will have a long-term programme, it is likely that its membership will change over time. It is therefore important to elect at least two members who are committed to remaining in the working group throughout its active phases and ensure that people who have to leave the group are replaced.

Once the working group is convened, they will need to learn as much as possible about areas to be addressed by the policy. This could be done by reading, through discussion with acknowledged 'experts' or by attending training events. The next step will be to identify their own beliefs, values and principles in relation to the policy area and reflect upon these in the light of their knowledge of the policy area to be developed. What are the values they are trying to promote? Are they reasonable? What degree of consensus exists within the working group? Once they feel they know sufficient to lead the school in the policy development process they can begin to plan for the first year. Over the year every member of the school community – students, staff and parents – should have opportunities to learn about the issue to be tackled, to explore and possibly challenge their own values and attitudes in relation to this and to discuss what the policy should consist of. Events and meetings which are already timetabled will provide opportunities for achieving this. Additional meetings and events can be planned well in advance. Providing training for staff helps them to feel more confident in discussing the issue to be addressed by the policy with the students and parents. They will also have begun to examine their own values relating to the topic and to align themselves with the consensus values which will underpin the policy.

All staff can be involved in the process of consultation with students and parents. This makes policy development a high profile theme for the whole school and communicates the message that this is something the school takes very seriously.

Developing the policy

Developing the policy requires discussion, training and consultation. In the DfE Sheffield anti-bullying project, the schools which involved all staff and students in extensive training and discussion of bullying behaviour and consultation over how it could be prevented and responded to had the biggest reductions in levels of bullying and the largest increases in numbers of students who were willing to tell a teacher if they were having a bad time in school. Schools which did not involve all staff and students had little impact on behaviour. By involving everybody in the process of policy development schools encourage a sense of collective responsibility for implementing it.

Through training and discussion it is possible to increase motivation to do something about the problem. This is particularly important for staff who are going to need to put considerable energy into implementing and maintaining the policy in practice. The process of consultation will inform the guidelines prepared by the working group. Through consultation, consideration should be given to the role students, parents and staff can play in implementing the policy. If the policy only refers to staff behaviour, it will imply that implementing the policy is a staff responsibility. This may be the case with some policies but those policies which relate to pastoral and social welfare in the school such as behaviour, equal opportunities, tackling bullying, inclusion of children with special educational needs are everybody's responsibility. Policies which address these aspects of school life will have implications for staff, students and parents and therefore they all need to be involved in the development process.

The ideas of the whole school community about what the policy should consist of are collated by the working group and included in a draft policy.

Policy contents

A policy should contain:
- the aims of the school
- definite guidelines for immediate and long-term action in order to achieve the aims
- procedures for monitoring the success of the policy
- implications of the policy for the behaviour of staff, students and parents.

The policy will need to be written in clear, accessible language which is appropriate for all those people who will be expected to implement it. In the DfE Sheffield anti-bullying project some teachers worked with primary aged students to translate the policy into their own 'rules for our class'.

Implementing the policy

The policy should shape staff and student behaviour throughout the school. If this does not happen we have to ask ourselves why. There are a number of reasons why individuals may not implement the policy. These include:
- lack of understanding and knowledge;
- lack of skill;

• lack of motivation.

All of these can be addressed by the management team on an individual or group basis as appropriate. Lack of understanding, knowledge and skill can be addressed through training. Maintenance of the policy over time will depend upon a continuous programme of curriculum work and skills training for both students and staff.

Lack of motivation may arise because the individual aspires to values which are not reflected in the policy. If this is the case then the lack of motivation can be addressed by providing good reasons for implementing the policy. We will use the example of the anti-bullying policy to illustrate this. For some people, understanding how badly an individual may be affected by bullying and violence is sufficient to motivate them to take action. This is probably because they hold a value about not hurting others intentionally. For others, the hindrance of educational progress or whole school performance will be a motivator. These people may have values which relate to the importance of education and it will be important for senior managers who wish to motivate these people to demonstrate that bullying can have negative effects on learning and that tackling the problem will lead to improved opportunities for learning. For a few, motivation to implement the policy will be achieved through identifying and monitoring personal behaviour targets and regular performance review. These latter individuals may never be committed to tackling bullying and violence but will implement the policy because it is part of their responsibility to do so. A key to motivating staff will be to understand their key values in relation to education and also with regard to the issue to be addressed by the policy.

Regular communication of the whole school policy is essential for maintenance. Behaviour is slow to change and most people need first to be taught how to behave differently and then to be rewarded for doing so. Whilst new behaviours are being learnt, frequent reminders are necessary.

Evaluation of the policy

How does a school know whether or not a policy works in practice? Evaluation of a policy can occur along three dimensions:

• how well do staff and students know the policy?
• how effectively does the policy achieve what it sets out to do?
• how satisfied are staff, students and parents with the policy in practice?

Indicators relating to these three dimensions can be developed. Once the indicators have been agreed then ways of collecting information about them can be established. This information can be gathered qualitatively and quantitatively by using survey methods or by reviewing relevant records kept by the school.

In relation to bullying, indicators might include:

• reduction in the number of reported incidents of violence and bullying reduction in the duration of bullying

- reduction in the number of more serious incidents of violence and bullying
- increase in the number of students willing to tell a teacher if somebody is being nasty to someone else
- increase in the number of students who would be willing to help someone who is the victim of violent behaviour
- increase in the number of students and parents who believe the school takes positive action against bullying and violence.

Indicators of improvement in meeting the special educational needs of individual students might include:

- successful achievement of targets set in individual education plans and at annual reviews of statemented children
- increase in the number of students who make reverse progress through the stages of the Code of Practice e.g. from stage 3 to stage 2; from stage 2 to stage 1 etc.
- earlier identification of children experiencing difficulty and greater range of differentiation available within the classroom setting
- increase in parental attendance at stage 3 reviews
- increase in the number of parents of children with special educational needs who wish to send their children to the school.

The outcomes of policy evaluation will enable the school to review its policy. Values change and develop over time and therefore policy review will need to take account of new thinking and beliefs.

Do policies really make a difference?

Clear evidence of the effectiveness of whole school policies in changing attitudes and behaviour emerged from the DfE funded Sheffield anti-bullying project. In primary schools levels of bullying fell by as much as 80 per cent, with an average of 15 per cent overall. Across all phases 12 per cent fewer students said they had bullied someone else. The biggest reductions in bullying behaviour coincided with the work within the school on policy development, suggesting that it was indeed the policy work which contributed to these changes. In secondary schools 38 per cent more students said they would tell someone if they were being bullied. Fifteen per cent of students said they would not join in bullying someone and 31 per cent more students said they would help a fellow student if they saw they were being bullied. The changes in behaviour and attitudes were greater in schools which had most actively involved all staff and students. Follow-up studies in the primary and secondary schools (Eslea and Smith 1994; Thompson 1995) have suggested that the impact of the policy continues over time if there is regular discussion and training for both staff and students. The importance of involvement throughout the process of policy development and maintenance was further emphasised by comments of teaching staff:

I think the best session we had was when we sat down as a whole staff in small groups. We talked about what we thought bullying was and what we could do about it. It really brought out the cynics and changed most staff's genuine concern into an anger: why should these people get away with making other people's lives a misery? There was so much energy to do something about it.

It's made such a difference – we really are together now – there is a sense of solidarity and agreement. At the beginning everyone had different views ... some people didn't care ... they thought it was a joke, like ... and now we all know what to do and believe what we are doing is right.

... and the kids were consulted. They felt really good about that. We actually talked about the fact that this identified it as a really important document for the school ... they took it as a really important task and came up with all sorts of comments ... this has been different and good.

It's something that's going to have to be kept to the fore – so that it filters through – rather than something that we've done and that's it.

The results of the DfE Sheffield anti-bullying project suggest that establishing a policy can shape not only behaviour but also values and attitudes. However, the study is absolutely clear that it is not the policy itself which makes the difference but rather the process through which it is developed and maintained.

The central role of values in establishing a policy

Is it possible to develop a whole school policy which does not reflect a core set of values? Probably not. If the policy is to be effective then the beliefs, values and principles it is based on must be explicitly articulated. If this does not happen, the school runs the risk of having a policy which runs contrary to the core values promoted by the school. Alternatively a significant number of the people expected to implement the policy may have different values and therefore will misinterpret the policy, ignore it or at worst undermine it (Thompson and Sharp 1994).

Policies which are based on clearly articulated beliefs, values and principles are more likely to be implemented. They provide a framework, a set of guidelines which enable people working in the school to make their own decisions which uphold those values important to the school. They therefore enable autonomy and independence without compromising consistency of practice. They provide a sense of cohesiveness and belonging – an identity unique to the school which enables people from different and diverse communities to work constructively and purposefully together in one community – the school.

Chapter 8

Are We Ready for Inclusion?

Geoff Lindsay

The question which serves as the title to this chapter addresses the essence of special needs education. Despite the development of the past hundred years and more, both in legislation and educational practice, we do not have a fully inclusive system of education. Some argue forcibly that this lack is an affront to the human and civil rights of a significant minority of our children and young people; others argue that we are not ready but that potentially we could be, given various resources; a third group argue that we can never have a totally inclusive system, either on grounds of finance or practicality, and the aim is to optimise the system to balance obligations to those with special educational needs (SEN) against obligations to the rest of the population.

In this chapter I shall argue that this debate is ultimately about values: those values that are implicated in any discussion of inclusive education and how these interact with questions of evidence. I shall argue that too frequently the debate has not clearly separated these two different though interacting factors: value and evidence.

Integration and inclusion

First it is necessary to address the meaning of terms which are used in this discussion: integration and inclusion, in particular, but also others which are used in this domain, particularly mainstreaming and normalisation.

It is important to recognise that word meanings can be slippery. Terms which were once used in normal conversation are removed as awareness of their meaning increases. Unthinking use of the male gender in language has given way to non-sexist language; terms such as subnormal, idiot, imbecile, once 'technical' terms in the sense that they were defined operationally, have dropped out of usage as they have been recognised as offensive. The position with integration–inclusion is analogous in some respects, but not others.

An important factor to consider is historical time. In general, integration has been the term in general use among educationists, particularly through the 1960s–80s. This reflected the reality of the education system. Some children were excluded from mainstream schools and placed in segregated 'special' schools. Furthermore, until 1971 some children were deemed 'ineducable' and excluded from the education system altogether. During the past 20 to 30 years, therefore, there was an emphasis on de-segregation. This has resulted in two processes. Firstly, the promotion of children in special schools being transferred (integrated) into mainstream schools. Secondly, increasing resistance to removing children from the mainstream in the first place. Both of these processes, one remediative the other preventative, were considered examples of integration in that individual children with SEN were placed within a host culture, the mainstream school. Support for this on the part of child, parents, teachers and other professionals might vary, but the effect was the same: individual children were 'absorbed'. In practice, however, there were at least four issues that arose.

Motivation

Motivation for integration has been based on different values. For some it represented the promotion and realisation of a fully comprehensive system of education. Others were concerned that a child in segregated provision would necessarily receive an inferior education by being outside the normal system.

Receptivity of the school

Research on teacher attitudes to integration has shown some generally consistent findings (see Clough and Lindsay 1991, especially Chapter 11). Teachers have expressed a cautious welcome for integration and this appears not to have varied much over a period of nearly 40 years. Scruggs and Mastropieri (1996) report, on the basis of 28 studies from 1958–95 that, generally, two thirds of general classroom teachers supported mainstreaming–inclusion. On the other hand teachers have been more positive about certain types of disability (e.g. physical disability) than others (e.g. emotional and behavioural difficulties). They have also been more positive about integration in principle and therefore in the abstract, but less so for their own classroom and hence in reality. Concerns about their lack of expertise and training, and the need for other resources have been common.

However, despite their concerns, many schools have been positive and indeed proactive, as the following example indicates:

> Valley School was a school of about 150 children with a new nursery, so allowing children to stay in this community school from 3½–11 years. The headteacher was the parent of a young man with severe learning disabilities. He had supported earlier initiatives in setting up a separate Centre where primary aged pupils with a variety of learning difficulties

could receive more intensive help on a short term basis (1 to 2 years), while remaining on their school roll and then returning to their schools after this period. The head was keen to support the establishment of a provision in the nursery for 10 children with a variety of SEN, and the later extension of this resource for an extra 10 children at primary age.

Discussions with him revealed that his rationale was based fully on his belief that all children should be educated within their community. Given that not all schools at that time could support all children, he would provide an Integrated Resource where children with significant SEN could be educated in a mainstream, if not always their local school.

Concern of other schools

Any change can be interpreted as producing winners and losers. In addition to the children being integrated, this notion could apply to other parts of the system. Special schools losing children become unviable; professionals in those schools, or working to the previous orientation, might see their practice, their values and their jobs attacked. This is not a necessary correlate of change. Some teachers in special schools welcomed the developments from a shared sense of philosophy, while others decided this was the likely scenario for the future and to go along with it.

During the early 1970s the assessment practice in LEAs changed. Instead of a school medical officer 'ascertaining' a child's 'disability of body or mind', educational psychologists and teachers were also brought into the process, which gradually shifted from being medically to educationally organised. (At the same time, the approach shifted from medical to psychoeducational conceptualisation.)

Change in one LEA was dramatic. Over the period of 1 to 2 years the psychologists failed to refer children for placement in special schools (known at the time as ESN(M): educational subnormal (moderate) and generally comparable to current designation of moderate learning difficulties). There was an outcry from the ESN(M) schools, backed later by other special schools. The best part of a year group had not been referred, it was argued. In a few years, schools' viability would be threatened. Interestingly, the discussion focused on the view that ESN (M) children existed, that they needed placement in ESN (M) schools and so the psychologists were disadvantaging the pupils.

Finance

Before Local Management of Schools (LMS) and Local Management of Special Schools (LMSS) the financial support for children with SEN was clearly with the LEA (together with the health service). The LEA developed new special schools, or not; developed more integrated provision, or not. Since LMS and LMSS the issue of finance has increased in visibility. All schools are now aware of the money coming into their budget for SEN under the LMS formula. They can also see how much, in total, goes into the special schools system, and to individual schools, or integrated provision.

> The head of a large secondary school was supportive of the LEA setting up an Integrated Resource for children with moderate learning difficulties. He was committed to the children being as fully integrated into the school as possible and consequently, while there was a base, all the pupils attended ordinary lessons, often with support, for varying amounts of time.

> Under LMS this head noted the financial worth of pupils attending the LEA's special schools. This varied both in terms of the severity of the special needs catered for, as might be expected and accepted, but also with respect to the school's 'efficiency'. For example, if a school with places, and hence staffing and other resources, for 60 children has only 45 pupils on the roll, the unit cost for each of these children rises. Also, as the unit cost is much higher initially anyway, such increases are greater than would be found in mainstream schools with unfilled places.

This head teacher argued that this school would be prepared to accept more of these children currently segregated, *but* there should be similar financial support to that currently spent on special school children for those in his Integrated Resource.

These examples indicate the factors influential in supporting or resisting integration. However, there is a fifth issue which concerns the *effectiveness* of the provisions available, whether integrated or segregated. Irrespective of the motivations, wishes and philosophies of key agents, it is possible to base decisions also on relative benefit in educational terms, defined widely or narrowly. This dimension will be addressed below.

Types of integrated provision

Integration–segregation may be characterised as a continuum from total forms of either provision to variants which fall in between. The types of provision developed over the past two decades may be characterised differently, but the following are key elements.

Total segregation

The child is educated entirely in a separate educational provision. This may be, at its most extreme, a provision removed from the rest of the society where the child has been deprived of his or her liberty owing to legal restraint or psychiatric action owing to a mental illness. More commonly, the child is in a special school either in residence or as a day-pupil, but the only interaction with children outside the school is social, and most commonly organised by the family or carers when the child is at home. In the past, many long-stay hospitals for children and young people with significant learning disabilities have been effectively segregated to a high degree, at least for some pupils.

The argument for such a provision is that it allows a focus of expertise with children having low incidence disabilities and needs and that it is therefore more effective educationally, and more cost effective. On the other hand in the traditional typology such a provision is seen as clearly one to be avoided on grounds of segregation from the rest of society. However, there are those, in particular some of the deaf community, who have argued in its favour for some children. In particular, a residential school for the deaf may provide a positive environment for some deaf children, particularly where deaf adults and children develop and use their agreed sign language as a means of communication. Otherwise this degree of segregation is usually unpopular and considered an affront to the child's rights to be able to develop with children without SEN.

The special base and integration

A second type of provision places the child in a special school, but with activities undertaken in mainstream. In the past this has generally taken the form of children based in a special school undertaking occasional, usually social, activities with other children in mainstream. However, there are two variants:

- special school, with child or groups visiting other schools for planned activities with educational goals
- special unit within a mainstream school, from which the child attends lessons in other parts of the school.

Note that in practical terms, i.e. what happens in the classroom, these could be equivalent. If the educational experiences are planned and supported successfully then whether the base is a separate school, some distance away or on the same campus, or a unit within another school, may be a matter of organisation only.

However, research has suggested that social interaction between children with SEN and others may occur more often during the social periods, including simply moving around the school (e.g. Murray-Seegert 1989).

Mainstream school with integrated resource

Here the child is a member of the main school which has a Resource base. Typically the Resource is planned and, in the past, was funded direct by the

LEA, and may comprise from 5 to 10 up to 30–40 pupils, depending on the size of the school and the nature of SEN addressed. Depending upon levels of resourcing as well as need, the children may spend varying amounts of time in the base and the mainstream school. In some cases the 'base' is a clear entity, with a physical location, equipment etc.; in other cases the Integrated Resource is more ephemeral with the children being supported entirely in class.

> Highlands School has an integrated resource with three small rooms and three teachers. The pupils all have severe and profound hearing loss and vary across levels of attainment with some reading at several years below age level when they enter the school at 11 years, to children who obtain a high number of GCSE grade A–C passes. Two of the rooms serve as a social as well as teaching bases for all the pupils, but the time spent here for lessons varies from pupil to pupil, from zero to over half the week. In rare cases more flexibility is provided. For example John had moved into the LEA having been out of school for several months. A period of highly supported 'settling in' was possible, with John spending most of his time in the base, before gradually extending his time in mainstream lessons. For the majority of pupils most lessons take place in mainstream with some supported by a teacher of the hearing impaired; other lessons, mainly intensive language work or preparation and follow-up for other subjects take place in the base.

Mainstream school

The first variant is the mainstream school which takes an individual child and engineers the integration of that child into the school community. Government statistics suggest that the majority of children on statements are now integrated as individuals into mainstream schools rather than attending special school (Office of Her Majesty's Chief Inspector 1996c), although it is not possible to know whether this represents a higher proportion of children who would previously have been in special schools, or a widening of the definition of 'severe and complex needs' to give statements to a broader population of children e.g. those with specific learning difficulty–dyslexia. (The latter is more likely given the increase in the percentage of children with statements.)

> Chris was first referred by his speech therapist owing to a severe speech and language difficulty. He attended an Integrated Resource nursery receiving speech and language therapy in school as well as nursery experience. At five years he transferred to his local infant school. Chris was a child with autistic spectrum difficulties. His speech improved greatly and he became articulate. His language had many indications of advanced development, but he had difficulties with certain more subtle

aspects. His attainments were very good, in the top ten per cent or better. However, he continued to have difficulties with social awareness and relationships, and with behaviour, particularly his obsessions with sameness and conformity. His head teacher was highly experienced and supportive and the school was well ordered and positive. Staff also liked Chris and addressed his difficulties (often regarded as eccentricities) in a supportive manner. For example, a very good reader and with an advanced knowledge of time, Chris would call out in afternoon assembly, 'It's 3.15 Mrs Daniel,' if the head went a second over her intended session.

These examples of integration reflect the variety of models which have developed. They share, however, the common characteristic – that in all cases the child is integrated *into* a system. The 1981 and now the 1993 Education Acts, despite their requirements regarding the child being educated in mainstream school, have tended to set this system more rigidly. Whereas once some schools would simply take in a child as a local, 'one of ours', increasingly schools look to extra finance to accompany the child in order to enhance provision.

From integration to inclusion

From the preceding section it is clear that I do not consider there to be a simple definition of 'integration'. All of these models, and their sub-models are forms of integration, with variations on a number of dimensions: location of main base; amount and proportion of time; individual integration in a class, or with a special teacher or non-teaching assistant providing support; individually in a school, or into a designated Resource. In addition there are issues of the nature of the child's needs, including severity, domain and possible impact on other children. However, I would argue that the main process in most cases has until recently been one of integration. What, then, is inclusive education? Is it synonymous?

In my view, inclusive education is essentially a system which is based on a different premise from that of integration. With the latter, the education system exists and the child is negotiated into it. The onus is on the child fitting into the main system. This is not to argue that the system is necessarily inflexible or unwelcoming, it may be the exact opposite, but the child starts with no automatic right to be in mainstream. Inclusive education, on the other hand, starts from the child's right to belong. The assumption is that the education system is inclusive and hence there is no *requirement* that any child's right of entry be negotiated. This position is summed up well in the booklet describing the development towards inclusive education in Newham:

> The ultimate goal of Newham's Inclusive Education policy is to make it possible for every child, whatever special educational needs they may

have, to attend their neighbourhood school, and to have full access to the National Curriculum and to be able to participate in every aspect of mainstream life and achieve their full potential. (Newham Council undated, p.3.)

The Newham experience is informative in many ways. It is clear that the development towards integration and later inclusion was resisted by many, including parents of children with SEN as well as those who saw such children as threatening their own children's education. Also the authors stress that no overnight change is possible, and indeed that they did not seek this. However, if the intention of inclusion is accepted as the organising principle then this should influence a wide variety of development in education, not simply 'special education'. For example, the need or opportunity to build a new school requires a consideration of inclusive practice from the outset, not as an addition to mainstream developments.

The case for inclusion – is it made?

Rights

The arguments which drive moves towards inclusive education are largely of one type, namely rights – human and legal. The former argument is based largely on social and ethical concerns, and hence is directly related to values. In particular, there is a powerful argument, well supported by evidence, for the discrimination by society against those of its member with disabilities or SEN. This is broader than education. For example, Pfeiffer (1994) has outlined the history of the Eugenics Movement in the United States and details past and existing state laws which are discriminating. He argues that by 1930 thirty-three states had enacted involuntary sterilisation laws. Even today, he maintains, it is possible, legally, for involuntary sterilisation to be effected:

If a superintendent or county director can convince a judge that a person with a disability cannot manage day-to-day affairs, needs guidance, and would 'benefit' from sterilisation, then the judge can order that it be done. (p.484)

Pfeiffer gives other examples of the restriction and removal of human rights suffered by people with disabilities, and argues that these include segregation from mainstream society. He argues for support of the American with Disabilities Act (P.L. 101–336) as a step in the right direction.

In the UK there is equal concern for the rights of people with disabilities, and similar criticism of the system in operation. Barnes and Oliver (1995), for example, report that since 1982 there had been thirteen unsuccessful attempts to get anti-discrimination legislation through Parliament. While focusing mainly on adults they also argue that the then current Bill contained, 'no clauses promising disabled children and students the same rights as non-disabled peers; i.e. the right to be educated in mainstream schools and colleges'. (p.114)

Consideration of rights is not simple, however. We need to ask questions such as: Whose rights? Who decides what these rights are? What should be the priority for assuring their rights are recognised in law, and of ensuring they are respected in practice?

The first question may appear straightforward: surely these are the rights of the child with a disability or special educational need? But these children do not exist as a clearly defined sub-group, rather there are continua of disabilities and needs. Furthermore, there are trenchant criticisms of models of disability (see Chapter 2). Finklestein, for example, in a letter to *The Psychologist* (August 1996) was highly critical of the paper by Marie Johnson (1996) for ignoring the discussion of models of disability, in particular for ignoring the perspectives of disabled people: 'The WHO model of disability has been criticised by just about every disabled academic in his country since it first appeared' (p.342). Furthermore, there is a need to consider the rights of children *without* disabilities. The 1993 Education Act para. 160 requires children to be 'educated in a school which is not a special school unless that is incompatible with the wishes of his parent' if certain conditions are satisfied:

(2) The conditions are that educating the child in a school which is not a special school is compatible with:
   a) his receiving the special educational provision which his learning difficulty calls for
   b) the provision of efficient education for the children with whom he will be educated, and
   c) the efficient use of resources.

This issue came to the fore in 1996 with the cases of children allegedly exhibiting disruptive behaviour to a degree that permanent exclusion was required. Reports of leaders of teacher unions and other education figures revealed the 'needs of others' argument being promoted above the needs of the individual.

For example, the President of the Society of Education Officers, Heather de Quesney, was reported in the *Times Educational Supplement* (1 November 1996) as telling the annual conference of the Association of Educational Psychologists:

Public concern about social cohesion and the massive problems facing the whole of society demand more of us than the bland inclusive philosophy promoted in the past ... we must recognise the world for what it is rather than as we would like it to be. (p.2)

This leads to the question of who determines rights. In the end, legal rights are defined by Parliament and by case law in the courts. Neither system is renowned for its inclusion of people with significant disabilities. But legal rights develop, at least in part, from consideration of human rights, based upon social, moral and ethical considerations. Whereas traditionally this debate has been conducted by the able-bodied on behalf of those with disabilities, increasingly the voices of the latter are being raised and heard.

For children, however, there is a further complication. Younger children and those with significant intellectual impairment are restricted in their ability to appreciate the issues. Their parents have legal responsibility for their welfare, but are parents always in the best position to identify the appropriate rights for their child? In most cases, the parent will not have a disability, although the deaf community is a special case where many, but still a minority, of children with a significant hearing loss will have deaf parents. The prioritisation of legislation is, ultimately, a political process. Governments have legislative programmes based upon their particular ideologies (see Chapter 2) but need to determine priorities according to expediency, points scoring against the opposition, and keeping their party together, as much as by the manifesto programme. The influence of different factors will be determined by the strength of the leadership and degree of common thinking among the party. By 1997, the Conservative party's programme was being prosecuted not only with respect to the merits of the individual issues but against open criticism of the leadership, clear splits over Europe, and no overall majority. As a result, Bills with general support became battlegrounds for the settling of other scores.

The record for disability legislation is not good, as Barnes and Oliver have argued (see above) and the prioritisation of such legislation depends greatly on the pressure put to bear on government by the disability groups, professionals and individuals (Peter 1995). Increasing frustration is now leading to direct action by people with disabilities.

But even if laws are enacted their implementation may not be forceful. The failure of many LEAs to offer statements to children with SEN, or make appropriate provision to meet needs, was a matter of great concern after the 1981 Act. The introduction of the Special Educational Needs Tribunal system has been a clear attempt to meet these criticisms and the most recent report of the Tribunal shows the extent to which it has required LEAs to address children's special needs (see Chapter 2).

To return to my main theme, inclusive education, the previous discussion has highlighted that determining any right is not straightforward. Can we agree that inclusive education *is* a right? Clearly there are protagonists among professionals and people with disabilities themselves for whom the answer is self-evident. Any alternative to inclusive education is inherently inferior as it violates the basic right of a child to be educated in not only a mainstream setting, but the local community school. To achieve this will require large amounts of finance. For example the analysis by Coopers and Lybrand (1993) suggested that pupils with physical disabilities have access to all teaching space in only 26 per cent of all primary and 10 per cent of secondary schools.

Provision of adequate toilet facilities in all primaries would cost £59 million.

There is also a need for training of teachers and other education staff, and attitude change. But, while these will take time, if the rights of a child with a disability can only be met in an inclusive school, so be it. This appears to be the long-term policy of Newham, as exemplified by their mission statement, quoted above. However, this mission statement is based on the assumption that the elements it contains are necessarily linked, and individually as well as collectively the best options to meet the children's needs. The policy is reported to have widespread appeal, but is essentially silent on the *purpose* of this 'ultimate goal'. Inherent, and taken for granted, is that these operational targets are good in themselves. But can we assume this?

Evidence

A second approach to considering inclusive education is to start with a clearer set of goals which we want children to achieve. For example, rather than 'to attend their neighbourhood school' we might specify that children with SEN should 'form friendships and enjoy social relationships with their peers'. Rather than 'have full access to the National Curriculum' we might specify that the children 'achieve academic success across all subjects in the National Curriculum'. The latter could be sharpened by adding 'to their age level as a minimum', for example. This is not to criticise the Newham mission statement: this is a clear and therefore helpful statement of intent. But it is concerned with means rather than ends.

However, if we take this alternative approach, other questions arise. Do children need, necessarily, to attend their local school in order to develop friendships and general social awareness and competence? Clearly this is not the case as many children, particularly at secondary age, and also at nursery where there is less than 100 per cent coverage, travel across cities. The independent sector has children in residence from other parts of the country. Also, it is evident that not all children are happy at school, and that not all children have the ability to develop social skills and friendships without intensive support. Similarly some children may benefit academically from intensive work, not necessarily in a mainstream class. And there are some in the deaf community who believe that the abolition of the schools for the deaf are an attack on a coherent community, with its own language and social structure (e.g. Montgomery 1981).

It is therefore important to consider the evidence for the differential benefit of various forms of educational placement. Unfortunately, as reviews of such research have indicated, conclusions are not easy to draw as studies do not always compare like with like. For example, when comparing children placed in special and mainstream schools, can we be sure that the former were not so placed because their difficulties were considered to be greater? Also, the research in question has largely been carried out on systems of integration rather than inclusion, and in different countries, and so the findings might not apply to a truly inclusive system. Given these caveats, what does the research show? And what reliance can be placed on these findings?

Academic achievement

Reviews of research by Madden and Slavin (1983) and Lindsay (1989) suggest that children in special schools do not necessarily achieve greater academic success than those in integrated provision. However, the corollary is also true: integrated provision was not found to be clearly better than special schools. Subsequent studies have been more positive. For example, Sloper *et al.* (1990) in a study of 117 children with Down's Syndrome reported that:

> Children in mainstream schools were likely to have the highest attainment, followed by those in units in mainstream schools, MLD (moderate leaning difficulties) schools and SLD (severe learning difficulties) schools even after allowing for the difference in mental ages of the children in the different types of schools. (Parentheses added.) (p.291–2.)

However, the conclusion by Butler (1996), on the basis of studies in the United States, appears to be a reasonable generalisation:

> The move towards full inclusion is not based on a body of solid educational evidence demonstrating clear merits over special classes. Rather, what evidence there is seems to suggest that students do no worse in integrated settings and many do slightly better. (p.866.)

Social and emotional development

Earlier work I carried out with Masters' students suggested that simply integrating children with SEN into nurseries was not sufficient to achieve improved levels of social interaction (e.g. Lindsay and Desforges 1986; Lindsay and Dickinson, 1985). For example, in one study the most open-plan nursery had lower levels of interaction than a traditional box classroom, a setting where, in this school, the teachers had to engineer joint sessions between the children with SEN (normally in a separate room) and the mainstream nursery children.

Martlew and Hodson (1991) in a study of children with moderate learning difficulties in special schools and integrated resources within mainstream schools reported the children had fewer friends and experienced more teasing and bullying in the latter. They concluded that their findings did not give strong support to the beneficial aspects of integration, but that they did demonstrate negative aspects.

In a study in German-speaking Switzerland Bless and Amrein (1992) found pupils in integrated classrooms were less popular than those with no problems. Similarly, Sale and Carey (1995) in a study of a large inclusive school in the USA found that those children who were 'currently eligible' (i.e. would have had the equivalent of a statement), especially those with emotional and behavioural difficulties, were significantly more likely to be 'least liked' and significantly less likely to be 'more liked'.

Making sense of the research

This brief summary provides a flavour of the current position with regard to the empirical base for opinions regarding inclusive education. Put simply, but negatively, there is no compelling evidence from major studies to support inclusive education. However, as has been argued before (Lindsay 1989; Hegarty 1993; Booth 1996) this is not the way to approach the issue. Inclusive education is multi-faceted; the disabilities and needs of children are many and varied; the social systems within each country, and even within regions, set different contexts; judgements of better and worse beg questions regarding the variables to be chosen. However, while Booth appears sceptical of the place of research in inclusive education, I adopt a more positive stance. For example, there is now a literature of small-scale research using case study methodology which presents collectively a wealth of information regarding attempts to support children in mainstream settings. Not all is of good quality in the sense that the reports allow the reader a clear understanding of the context processes and outcomes. However, there are some very useful and interesting studies. I shall present just two as examples.

Carola Murray-Seegert (1989) conducted a study of a large inclusive high school in San Francisco which she claims was the first comprehensive high school west of the Rockies. The school has included students with disabilities since 1960, and offered a continuum from less to more restrictive learning environments (but all within the school) since 1981: regular class to self-contained special day class. In her study, Murray Seegert followed through 30 students with significant intellectual impairments. She presents a rich report detailing the life in school of the students over one year, with reference to the perceptions of staff, and the behaviour of the students. For example, she revealed the varying pattern of interaction between her group of students and other students in the school. She presents evidence that these are related both to the social structures among the whole student group and the focus students themselves. For example, those who regularly interacted appeared to be primarily from specific subgroups. None were on the school's honour roll; they tended to be in the 'least desirable' typology given by teachers; they were more frequently black and poorer financially than average for the school.

The account reveals not only differences in terms of frequency but also rich descriptions of life in the school. The result is an account which indicates both how well school can include its pupils and support their development, but also how complex this is. For example, although the school is regarded as inclusive, and clearly inclusive practice went on, there was much within-school separation which might be interpreted as exclusion.

The second study, by Salisbury *et al.* (1995) investigated the strategies used in an elementary school within the USA to promote social relations. Earlier studies have explored more specialised settings, but how will this be facilitated in a regular school with limited specialist help? Salisbury *et al.* examined 18 children, from Kindergarten to 6th Grade, and 10 teachers in 2 inclusive schools. They identified five themes considered important in supporting inclusion, based upon observation, interviews with teachers and focus group discussions.

First, the teachers engaged in active facilitation of social interactions. This replicated findings such as Lindsay and Desforges (1986) discussed above. However, also of interest, was that the teachers argued that their practice was 'the same as they did for all children', whereas the researchers argue they departed fundamentally from that, being highly involved in facilitating social interaction. For example, they were careful where they placed desks, to put the children in cooperative groups, to set collaborative problem-making activities. The teachers also spoke of using other pupils as a resource, 'turning it over to the kids' and intentionally worked to build a climate of concern for others. They also modelled acceptance: 'She's expected to participate, and she's expected to behave. It's obvious that we like her, and we're glad she's here, and she's included'. (p.134.)

Finally, specific policies and practices throughout the school were considered to support inclusion, including collaborative teaching and multi-age classrooms.

These studies are open to various criticisms but they each provide an example of inclusive education in practice. Each has its socio-cultural context, but we have deliberately chosen studies beyond the UK because we consider that despite this they each produce ideas which can be explored in this country. Each, therefore, provides evidence not on whether inclusive education works, or is better than segregational provision, but on how inclusive schools may operate, and some of the factors which must be addressed.

Conclusions

In my opinion we passed the point many years ago when questions about integration versus segregation were reasonable. Research cannot answer such questions. Rather, decisions about the macrosystem must be made primarily on the basis of values. What do we want for our children? I consider that all children should have their rights respected (see Chapter 10) and that one characteristic of a system which does this is that it is inclusive rather than exclusive. There are several specific issues. First, an inclusive system need not imply every school is inclusive. The latter may be an ideal, cutting down on travel, facilitating out of school contact, but it is possible to have a system which is inclusive but focuses resources. The current systems in Newham and Sheffield, for example, approach this (Newham LEA, undated; Lindsay *et al.* 1990).

Secondly, research is used to set up the basic system, and then to improve practice. We need clear evidence on buildings and the ecology of the school, but we also need to explore methods which facilitate classroom learning (e.g. special reading programmes; differentiated curricula) and social development (e.g. collaborative learning). In each case the need is to examine the contribution of the young person, teachers, other pupils, curriculum and ecology and their interaction. Also of importance is to engage the young person in the enterprise, from setting the questions to contributing evidence.

Thirdly, we need good evidence on the use of resources. This includes not only the benefits of particular forms of IT or aids to communication, for example, but also the way finance is allocated within schools. The latter is, of course, politically determined by central government and the construction of the budget formula for funding schools in each LEA. Given the powers allocated to schools to spend the 'SEN element' how they wish, subject to questions raised by parents or during an OFSTED inspection, we need to know how each school is prioritising its support for children with SEN.

Fourthly, we need to recognise that for any child there is a need to go beyond a position that asserts a 'right to inclusion'. Children deserve an education of quality. But there are real dilemmas in meeting needs. For example, the need to recognise parental rights and perspectives (Chapter 11) may require a variety of provision to meet their preferences. To remove special schools, for example, removes an element of choice, and as Roger Attwood and David Thompson show in Chapter 10 there are well argued reasons for settings other than a local school while resources, including expertise, are uncertain.

So, to return to the question posed in the title of this chapter. No, we are not ready for inclusion in the sense that many situations do not have sufficient resources, appropriate attitudes and history of good practice on which to build. But on the other hand, I believe there is no choice other than to develop inclusive systems of education which can then be improved by careful adoption of approaches based on evaluation of good practice.

Part 3

Values in Relationships

Chapter 9

Children's Developing Value Systems

Julie E. Dockrell

Do disabled people make you feel uncomfortable? If so, their greatest handicap could be you and your attitude. So, think of the person. Not the disability.
> (Poster for the International Year of Disabled People – 1981.)

The heaviest burdens of disability arise from personal interaction and not from the impairment itself. (Helen Keller.)

The values we hold about the desirability of means or actions, play a major role in the ways we interact with others and accept diversity. Helen Keller highlights the importance of broadening our conception of impairments to include the many obstacles that can arise because of the ways in which others understand these difficulties, interact with the individuals concerned and accept variation. Children's behaviour, just like that of adults, is influenced by the beliefs they hold and the knowledge they have. The focus of this chapter is children's developing value systems, how they come to understand and hold particular sets of beliefs and attitudes. In particular it will examine how children come to understand and accept variation in the behaviour and performance of their peers. I will argue that the ways in which children understand and conceptualise special needs will be influenced by the overriding value systems in their schools, families and society at large as well as their own ability to understand needs and differences. In parallel, social norms, past habits, experiences, and attitudes will determine behaviour towards others and children's views of themselves.

My aim in this chapter is twofold. Firstly, to consider the factors that influence children's value systems in a developmental framework. Secondly, to consider the ways in which children with and without special educational needs develop an understanding of special needs. When we consider development, it is always helpful to clarify what we think is developing. If we do not, it becomes difficult to isolate the processes and factors involved. Little, if any, work has been carried out investigating the acquisition of value systems. This results in a particularly problematic domain of inquiry. As we shall see research has focused on issues that are relevant to our understanding of children's value systems but no coherent model, theory or set of guidelines for development exists.

Value systems can be thought of as higher order sets of beliefs. They are not single statements, or necessarily moral statements; rather, they permeate the ways in which we think about problems and address issues. For example, a society which values conventional academic achievement above all other skills and behaviours will transmit this directly in the classroom. This will occur in terms of accepted work and often in terms of individual standing and worth. An interesting, and often unstated, aspect of value systems is that they differ. Value systems can differ between individuals, communities and cultures. Specific sets of values underlie different political systems, ideological beliefs and cultural mores. Consider the School Curriculum and Assessment Authority's recent consultation of values in education and the community. They note that the value statements they propose are 'not a definitive and complete list of the values people hold. By their nature they may not include those distinctive of particular religious or cultural groups' (School Curriculum and Assessment Authority 1996: p.2). Moreover the forum agreed ' that there could be no consensus on the source of the values that we all share or how to apply the values that we all share' (p.6). Thus unlike other areas of development such as reading, number and social skills there is no absolute end point to which children must aspire. Yet OFSTED (1994) suggests that pupils provide evidence of moral behaviour that among other things demonstrates personal values in relation to self and others, and to local, national and world issues.

The value systems that underlie education and educational practice can affect children in two distinct ways. In the first place they provide a model from which children can derive their own views, beliefs and values. Secondly they directly impact on children in terms of the experiences they receive and the views they develop about themselves and others. Identifying the ways in which children develop a value system is of major importance for educators, cares and professionals alike. One thing we can be sure of is that children's values do not come from simply being told to behave in particular ways or believe particular doctrines. The communication occurs in a wider context and, as developmental psychologists have learnt in other areas, this context is of major importance. Development occurs as the result of the interaction between the child and other people (Sameroff and Chandler 1975). The development of a value system or systems does not take place in a social vacuum but within a particular set of social arrangements including families, communities and cultures. However, if there is no definitive universal set of values and values are not constructed by explicit instruction how do they develop?

Children's value systems

Developmental studies have had little to say about value systems. Instead they have either considered how children learn the difference between right and wrong, commonly called moral development, or focused on the processes by which children are helped to become responsible members of society (socialisation). Investigations of moral development have focused on the type of knowledge the children possess and their reasoning about moral dilemmas, while socialisation studies consider the factors that lead children to behave in particular ways. So, for example, studies have investigated children's evaluations of simple moral conflicts. Much can be learnt about developing values by considering what we know about moral development. Early theories of the development of moral judgement, such as those by Piaget and Kohlberg postulated stage-like progressions. Children were thought to move from an external source of morality and constraint (through authority figures) towards an autonomous morality based on cooperation, reciprocity, and understanding of human needs. Both changes in cognitive processes and social experience were thought to be central factors in this developmental pattern. As children become more sophisticated thinkers, they also refine the moral distinctions they make. These theories identify a major shift in children's views of the world from an egocentric view to a view that takes others' perspectives into account. It is argued that as a children grow older they are able to consider both the needs of others and the reasons why other children might not behave as they do. In practice this means that primary aged children (or children with cognitive skills at that level) will be unable to take someone else's perspective into account. So, in theory, a child would not be able to differentiate intentional hitting in the playground from accidental occurrences.

Such a stage-like progression would have major implications about the possibility (or not) of helping children understand and accept unpredictable or special behaviour. However, there are now many doubts about the idea that such judgements are *simply* a matter of better reasoning skills. For example, studies which focus only on factors that consider what is happening within the child fail to account for cross-cultural differences. Neither can they account for the fact that children make different judgements when asked to evaluate a situation from the position of self, a peer or a teacher, thereby demonstrating that they are capable of differentiating the perspectives of others. Moral development, itself, cannot be simply accounted for by a series of within child transformations.

An important distinction needs to be drawn between *social conventions,* such as the kind of clothes that must be worn to school, and *moral obligation* such as not destroying others' property. Moral transgressions are thought to be based on obligation, fairness and welfare while conventional transgressions are associated with authority, social nonconformity and social coordination. Young children distinguish more sharply between moral and conventional events for familiar rather than unfamiliar issues. With age, children are able to apply criteria to a broader range of social events. Development proceeds from reliance on specific personal experiences to an ability to abstract or generalise to unfamiliar events. However this distinction is not universal across cultures. Some cultures do not accept the idea that social practices are conventions and failure to adhere to food customs, etiquette and manners may be deemed to be moral transgression. The moral and the conventional develop alongside each other being modified by the context in which the children find themselves.

Value systems include both elements of the moral and conventional and they also include broader dimensions such as beliefs related to *higher order concepts* including respect for reasoning, a respect for truth, fairness, an acceptance of diversity and cooperation, justice freedom, equality, concern for the welfare of others, and peaceful resolution of conflict. Moreover, when we consider value systems, we must go beyond specific behaviours and focus on the factors that impact on the internalisation of aspirations and beliefs. Thus value systems are not simply deciding on the rightness or wrongness of a specific action, rather they are a complex set of beliefs which will be based upon a number of 'understandings' in the young child, including the notion of equity, understanding the needs and feelings of others, truth and falsehood as well as morality. Such understandings may or may not be demonstrated directly by the child's behaviour. For a variety of personal and external reasons beliefs may not translate into behaviour. A child might, for example, believe that bullying is wrong but hesitate to report or intervene in a bullying situation because of fear. Equally a head teacher may believe that the needs of all children should be met in a mainstream classroom but organisational constraints may mean that in this school total inclusion is not possible. Of course, any children who witness both of the above events will not necessarily be aware of the dilemmas. In sum, value systems encompass certain moral judgements but also include a broader range of judgements. These belief systems will frequently, but not always, be evident in children's behaviour and will underlie their attitudes and beliefs.

The developing mind

To unpack children's values we need to consider their behaviour in the context of both their beliefs and their understanding. Certain types of knowledge and understanding are necessary to make sense of the world. In developing a value system, how children understand each other's knowledge and intentions, their theory of mind and their ability to understand and interpret other children's competencies will all impact on the way they understand and reinterpret the world around them. Developmental theories of cognition have moved away from viewing cognitive development as a series of stage-like transitions and consider the child to be a much more active learner driven by their knowledge as well as the cognitive processes they possess. There are three dimensions that are of particular concern when we consider developing a value system. These are the *kinds of concepts* that a child has, the *complexity of the task* and the child's ability to *generalise to other situations*.

Concepts matter because they help us organise the world. There is strong evidence that infants are capable of a wide range of basic conceptual distinctions. As children grow older they begin to construct a representation of themselves in terms of category membership (such as gender) and their own unique characteristics and skills. Other people help define the child's uniqueness. Yet, in many ways children's drive to categorise themselves and others provides a ready-made basis for constructing social groups and deriving social valuations.

In parallel, the child's cognitive system deals with an increasing set of complex dimensions. For example, Piaget observed that young children failed to consider intentions when proportioning praise and blame; they tend instead to focus on objective outcomes. By contrast, older children will argue that an individual can take credit for, and should be rewarded for, only those outcomes which were intended. Damon (1975) demonstrated that four year olds equate justice with self-interest. By six years of age the notions of deserving appear and, by eight, weight is also given to differing needs. So eight year olds were able to give special consideration to the poor, for example. It is easy to see how this ability to consider different factors in such equations could influence children's acceptance of diversity and their views of their peers with special needs. Yet these cognitive changes do not occur in a vacuum. They are influenced by the social groups in which children find themselves and their own positions in the system. Emler and Dickson (1993) argue that children acquire those ideas that have currency and significance within the social environments they inhabit. The child's cognitive system will help support but not determine the dimensions that become meaningful for the child.

Contexts of development

To understand the beliefs that children develop and the attributions they make we need to address the contexts in which children find themselves. Yet the notion of context is very diffuse and on its own is not a helpful one. How can we come to understand this wider context and how might it impact on the child's fledgling value system? Bronfenbrenner (1979) has tried to specify more precisely what the nature of environmental influences on development might be. In Bronfenbrenner's theory of the *Ecology of Human Development* the environment is envisioned as a series of nested structures that extend beyond the immediate setting. Each level is thought to greatly affect the child. These levels are called the microsystem, the mesosystem, the exosystem and the macrosystem and are illustrated in Figure 9.1.

The first, and most local level, is called the *microsystem*. Bronfenbrenner defines the microsystem as: 'a pattern of activities, roles, and interpersonal relations experienced over time by the developing person in a given setting with particular physical and material characteristics' (p. 22). The microsystem

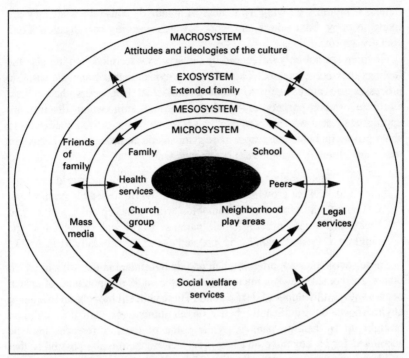

Figure 9.1 The ecological system: microsystem refers to relations between the child and the immediate environment; mesosystem refers to the network of interrelationships of settings in the child's immediate environment; exosystem refers to social settings that affect the child but do not directly impinge upon him or her; and macrosystem refers to the attitudes, mores, beliefs, and ideologies of the culture.

for children includes the places they inhabit, the people who live with them, the things they do together and their direct experiences. This means, of course that the children find themselves in many different microsystems – classrooms, friendships, playgrounds and so forth.

An important part of Bronfenbrenner's definition is that he emphasises both the physical setting and the relationships between the individuals in that setting. The social relations in a microsystem can determine the success or failure of the specific activities that occur. These relationships are bi-directional: the environment affects the child but equally the child affects the opportunities afforded by the environment. So, for example, in the second and third years of life children become increasingly aware of the norms in their families and communities that regulate behaviour. Such norms include both social conventions, such as remaining at the table during dinner, and moral imperatives such as refraining from violence against others. This increasing awareness of social conventions and moral rules leads young children to regulate their own behaviour and sometimes to police the behaviours of others. Children's growing awareness of standards constrain what they are likely to copy from others and work towards ensuring socialisation along socially approved lines.

Children are not only influenced by the acts they see modelled but also the feelings they see expressed. There is strong evidence that some socialisation processes are more likely to promote pro-social behaviours than others. Children whose parents are both warm and firm when disciplining appropriately, and who also provide their children with positive experiences to show pro-social behaviour, show more sympathetic and cooperative behaviour than other children. Dunn (1988) comments: Our

> conversational analyses show that the social rules of the world in which the children were growing up were continually discussed by the mothers: discourse on what was acceptable, what unacceptable, surrounded them...The moral order of their parents' world was conveyed to the children again and again in the repeated events of their daily lives. (p.73.)

These social rules are often implicit and demonstrated in the ways in which others are considered. An interesting example of the importance of match occurs with deaf children of deaf parents. These children brought up in signing environments do significantly better on all dimensions than deaf children brought up by hearing parents. While some of these differences may be accounted for by cognitive and linguistic factors, there is the possibility that children tune into an environment which affords a much wider range of opportunities and meshes with their own experiences.

Formal education provides children with a microsystem which offers both explicit and implicit beliefs to guide their construction of values. The explicit introduction of value statements occurs through Personal and Social Education in Britain, and in North America through a variety of packages. Children are encouraged and supported to become responsible citizens. The American Psychological Association Monitor (1995) recently reported the development of character education programmes where children are helped to understand and articulate shared values. It is important to ask whose values are being shared and articulated. Are they values that would be accepted by all cultural groups and all religions? If not how will children reconcile the conflict that may exist between what they are exposed to at school and what is expected at home?

Of equal concern for educationists ought to be the match (or not) between articulated values and the implicit messages passed through the curriculum and other actions. For example, Raven (1988) argued that:

> In the course of this research it has become clear that the presence or absence of relevant educational processes can be indexed by asking pupils about such things as what kinds of behaviours are valued by their fellow pupils and their teachers, what kinds of activity are encouraged and rewarded, whether they themselves are encouraged to do new things and decide for themselves what they will do, whether turning in a first-

rate performance is applauded and a second-rate performance frowned upon .....whether a wide range of pupils with different talents are encourage to develop and use them and whether those contributions are built on and recognised by others. (p.77)

Children will find themselves in a variety of relationships and settings which will foster views about society and their contribution to society. Of course, young people will not necessarily accept the values to which they are exposed but they will provide a frame of reference for the child to work within (or against).

Bronfenbrenner's next level, the *mesosystem*, acknowledges the importance of the relationship between these levels. Bronfenbrenner uses the term mesosystem to describe situations in which behaviour is a function of events that occur in more than one environment. Ideally, special provision should be designed as mesosystem models so clear links are set up between what the child experiences at home, for example, and what is occurring in school. From Bronfenbrenner's perspective, when microsystems fail to complement each other, then distancing or conflict is possible. The central principle here is that the stronger the links between settings, the more powerful the resulting mesosystem as an influence on the child's development. Such links can work well to support the child. An important protective factor for children who are poverty-stricken is their involvement in social networks that offer them support. In fact the number of non-relatives involved in their support and the number of different roles children play are predictors of positive adjustment. In contrast there are potential dangers when the views of the two systems are at odds. A study examining American mothers' views of their role in their children's learning illustrates this point well (Jarret 1993). Some teachers of the Afro-Caribbean children in this study believed that the children were not supported at home and for this reason did not learn in school, that their parents did not care and therefore that school resources were wasted on them. At the same time the parents expected schools to take full responsibility for their children's instruction. This mismatch in expectations has a direct impact on how the child is perceived but also may have an indirect impact on the support provided to that child.

Conflicts between microsystems are not necessarily negative, even though they may be difficult to negotiate. They may in fact result in significant learning experiences for the individuals involved. A mismatch between a school's expectation of a child's performance and familial expectation of a child's performance may alter expectations or views of the child and the conflict could be constructive. Young adults constantly tussle with the frequently contradictory value systems presented by their families and peers.

Bronfenbrenner's third level, the *exosystem*, is concerned with social settings that do not necessarily contain children but may nevertheless indirectly affect them, such as the workplace of the child's parents and local community services. Bronfenbrenner emphasises the importance of exosystem support on a child's development. For example, flexible work schedules, paid maternity and paternity leave, and sick leave for parents whose children are ill, are ways in which exosystem factors can affect a child. Consider the effect of public transport on children's welfare. If housing is not adequately served by a transport system it can limit a child's access to public health services, school and peer contact, and thereby influence the range of experiences and opportunities to which the child has access. Exosystems can, potentially, offer a range of supports which allows children and young people with special needs to participate fully in activities or they can serve to marginalise and distance them.

The last level of Bronfenbrenner's model is the *macrosystem*. It is not a specific environmental context but refers to the ideology and values of a culture, which affect decisions made at other levels of the model. As an example, consider the values that affect decisions about the educational provision for children with learning difficulties. The issue of whether children with learning difficulties should be educated in mainstream schools following, at relevant points, an individual programme designed to overcome their particular difficulties, or whether these children should be educated in special schools, is determined by a complex set of educational and economic factors, which reflect the values of a particular culture at a particular time (Wolfendale 1987). As other chapters in this book (especially Chapter 2) clearly illustrate British government legislation impacts on the educational opportunities for children with special needs.

Cultural beliefs can have a direct impact on the acceptability (or not) of certain patterns of behaviour. For example in cultures where infant and child mortality is high there are consequences for children's socialisation where the priority will be survival with an emphasis on compliant behaviour rather than a permissive regime. Thus practices that are valued by the community find legitimate expression in many ways. Such cultural values will also impact on what problems are seen as requiring special help (or not). In Britain, for example, children start to learn to read at the age of five; they are taught, and they spend much of their time practising reading at this age. Yet in other countries the appropriate age to start reading is seven. As Nunes (1994) argues:

> this difference although culturally determined is not without consequences for many children. In Britain a six year old can be labelled a 'backward reader' and be assigned to a remedial class whereas in Brazil or Sweden there is no room for such labelling at the age of six. (p.7)

Yet again there are other societies where school literacy is not valued highly at all.

Cultural values are portrayed in many ways and the media is a powerful messenger. There is much concern about the impact of television and the media on the beliefs and behaviours of young children. However, the focus of concern is, generally, around violence and sexuality. Little attention is paid to the ways in which special groups are portrayed and treated. Troyna (1981) states that ' For many people, the mass media represents a crucial source of beliefs and values from which they build up a picture of their social worlds'. The ways in which people with learning difficulties are depicted on television and in children's comics has a pervasive (and largely negative) effect. Yoshida *et al.* (1990) describe several studies which show how disabled individuals are portrayed more negatively than positively. They note the lack of coverage on the topic of special educational needs as opposed to other issues of social concern such as housing. In some cultures lack of exposure to the media and limited exposure to multiple values results in rumour and gossip providing a similar role.

The socio-cultural system in which the child grows up channels the development of cognitive as well as affective dispositions. Cultural differences can impact on what individuals consider to be fair and just. Consider the allocation of rewards. Rewards can be allocated by equality (all groups receiving the same), equity (with rewards being proportional to merit) or need (unequal rewards reflecting unequal needs). Striking cross-cultural differences are found when allocation of rewards is considered in experimental settings. American students favour an equity distribution, Cjines favour equality and Indians favour distribution in terms of need. With limited resources for special needs education one can see how views on resource distribution will have a major impact on the way the system is managed, and by corollary provide children with a socio-cultural infrastructure on which to hang their developing value systems.

Children's value systems and special educational needs

In this final section I consider what we know about children's understandings and beliefs about special needs. These beliefs are important because ultimately they will impact on their value systems and their views about fairness and equity. Moreover, there will be a link with the ways in which they treat their peers who are experiencing difficulties. The story for children who experience a special need is slightly different. For these children both their value systems and the ways in which they view (value) themselves as members of a class or peer group are being developed. There are two essential issues to consider when we are investigating children's perspective of special educational needs. Firstly, we need to address the content of the representations created by the individual children – what is it they believe? Secondly, we need to consider the factors that are thought to impact on these representations – how these representations develop. Each of Bronfenbrenner's levels is important but I will focus particularly on microsystems factors.

Children notice differences. Their cognitive skills allow them to mark certain aspects of diversity early and ultimately to construct concepts. Children as young as five classify able-bodied and physically disabled children into different groups and, as one would expect this understanding broadens and becomes more differentiated over the primary school period. By 6 years of age children are able to differentiate aggression from other behaviours whereas social withdrawal is recognised later, about 12 years of age (Safran 1995). Psychological problems are recognised later. The content of the associated representations is not predetermined but can quickly take on negative connotations..

Lewis and Lewis (1987) report that young six and seven year olds described their mainstream classmates who were seen as 'not very clever' and 'needing a lot of help' both in negative behavioural terms, e.g. self-inflicted difficulties, and negative cognitive terms e.g. as being slow. The general picture presented was that the children were not well-liked, wilfully misbehaved and therefore caused their own difficulties, and could change when and if they decided to. It appears that the more severe the handicap the more negative the attitude, but these attitudes are modified by the nature of the child's difficulty. This commonality may indicate that stereotypes are well-established in our society and may not be subject to simplistic modification. These negative views often become general representations in later years. Hastings *et al.* (1993) demonstrated that for 16 year olds, the vast majority of terms referring to special needs e.g. autism, SpLD, learning difficulties, dyslexia, are viewed negatively.

In fact the majority of studies show that there are significant differences between the status of disabled and non-disabled students in mainstream classrooms. Studies of children with general delays, specific learning difficulties, specific language impairments, hearing impairments and physical disabilities have all shown that these students experience peer rejection (Horne 1985). Moreover, there is a hierarchy of levels of peer acceptance. Physical difficulties are viewed the most positively followed by sensory, psychological and finally social–behavioural. This continuum is related to the age at which children begin to acquire the normative values of society and directly highlights the role of the macrosystem on children's behaviour. Interestingly *academic competence* was most highly associated with peer acceptance and *misbehaviour* was most closely related to peer rejection. It is hard to see how academic competence would be so highly valued unless this reflected the wider socio-cultural system. The issues surrounding emotional and behaviour problems may be different, however. Peers can play a prominent role in defining acceptable behaviour. Children show negative views of aggressiveness. Safran (1995) reports that student ratings indicate a significant negative correlation between peer acceptance and the following: outbursts, unprovoked aggression either physical or verbal, and indirect aggression. Further, the perceived negative impact of behaviour has been demonstrated to influence students' views of the difficulties experienced by children with special educational needs. These findings have implications for educators in improving acceptance and integration into mainstream settings.

Negative representations are present early. In many ways it is hardly surprising that such beliefs are formed given the wider negative societal view of disability and an emphasis on children as a set of exam results rather than as children, *per se*. These values transmitted from the macrosystem will often converge with the children's microsystem experiences (or lack of them). Yet, in many cases it is lack of experience and understanding that will support these negative connotations about their peers.

There is a general indication that experience results in more positive attitudes (see also Chapter 8). Children in integrated provision demonstrate more social concern and are more sociable with their peers with learning difficulties (Lewis 1993; Gash and Coffey 1995). Moreover, Gash and Coffey's data indicated that children who had experience of peers with learning difficulties showed flexibility about rules at playtime and were more likely to pick a child with a learning difficulty for their team. In contrast inexperienced children were less predisposed to sit beside, be best friends with or invite these children to a party. This is a forceful example of context enabling children to take the perspective of another and accommodating to their needs.

Better understanding of and added allowances towards problems come with increased age and contact. However, children's knowledge and understanding of special needs differs between children and would seem to be affected by a number of important factors – their age and cognitive sophistication, and the degree of contact, acquaintance and friendship with children who have special needs. Our own pilot work supports this view but also indicates that contact with one kind of difficulty can lead children to overgeneralise to other disabilities. It is not that children have inflexible views or are uninterested in special needs and diversity. Madge and Fassam (1982) argue that despite the interest shown by many of the junior school children to the concept of disability there was a lack of available information to enable this interest to be developed. Instead the content of the children's attitudes is derived from significant other sources and cultural products such as books, comics, television and videos: cultural products which often reflect extremely negative stereotypes.

However, exposure is not sufficient to change attitudes and behaviours: children's beliefs are influenced by the actual interaction patterns that occur. These interactions can be detrimental in terms of both peer acceptance and attitude formation. Interactions with perceived 'aggressive' students are likely to be more negative and ultimately have a negative impact on the 'special' child's inclusion in the day to day activities of the school (Safran 1995). Both positive staff attitude and class education are necessary to improve acceptance and ultimately help children value and understand diversity. Education may be particularly important for certain types of non-obvious difficulties (e.g. sensory) or for emotional and behaviour problems. In both cases interpretation of the child's behaviour needs to be contextualised for the specific behaviours to be understood.

Successful interventions to date point to a school level approach to values. Teachers are constantly transmitting values both through their behaviour and through what they teach. Teachers cannot conceal their outlook on life from their pupils and the academic material they teach has values embedded in it.

If disability is to be regarded as something normal then issues relating to impairment, disability and differences should be discussed as they arise. As Madge and Fassam (1982) argue:

> The goal of an entire education programme should be to foster interest in disability and to make everyone aware of the difficulties that these children face ... above all it should strive to demonstrate how very different the disabled are from one another and to make sure that preconceptions and stereotyped concepts are diminished. (p.142)

In sum the microsystem can go a long way to deconstruct wider societal representations and provide children with the beliefs and attitudes which will influence the value systems to which they will adhere. There is, however, little documented evidence that this occurs.

Children with special educational needs

Children with special needs are also in a position of developing value systems as well as locating themselves in a wider society. Children's perception of themselves and others depends on their majority or minority status in their community and on the quality of contacts they have with others. While not all which is not valued is devalued, many children with special needs are both marginalised and dis-empowered. This can occur in very subtle ways, such as who does the extra work with a child or how the child understands the assessment procedures which occur (Armstrong et al. 1993; and Chapter 6) and what their views are about the ongoing process, such as statementing (recording in Scotland).

There have been surprisingly few detailed studies carried out examining the self-concept of children with special needs. Moreover, there has been little consideration of the impact that these children's difficulties have on their own developing value systems. Children will vary in their experiences, expectations and ability to cope yet the data that are reported indicate that the children, on the whole, are characterised by lower self-concepts. Yet the relationship between academic performance and self-concept is not clear. Valuable information on the attitudes, experiences and needs of the children can be gained from asking questions. Where this has happened the children have welcomed the opportunity (Wade and Moore 1993).

Edwards (cited in Riddick 1995) presented detailed case studies of eight boys aged between 16–17 with dyslexia. What emerged was the amount of emotional suffering these boys experienced because of the reactions of teachers to their difficulties. These fell under four main headings – violence, unfair treatment, inadequate help and humiliation. In Riddick's own study half the children said they had been teased or called 'thick' at some point because of their dyslexia. The solution to this problem is not straightforward. The children found the label of dyslexia useful for themselves. They felt it indicated that they were not 'thick' or 'stupid', that there were other children with the same problem and that it helped them understand the problem. However, willingness to use the label in public was determined by other factors. One was the general attitude of the school. Half of the parents thought the teachers felt they were making an excuse for their child by calling him dyslexic.

The children's needs and experiences will also impact on the ways in which they understand societal rules and values. By virtue of their special status the children have different social experiences. Smetana *et al.* (1984) have shown how abused children considered psychological distress to be more universally wrong than neglected children, whereas neglected children considered the unfair distribution of resources to be more universally wrong than abused children. The children's increased sensitivity to the wrongness of transgressions was significantly influenced by the problems they had experienced.

Moreover, for some children it is important to alter our expectations. Moral and social rule distinctions among children with moderate learning difficulties are more akin to their developmental level. Such factors will need to be considered if the children's behaviours are to be understood in a developmentally appropriate fashion. Often, the impact of the child's problems is more subtle. Addressing a similar issue Ratchfurd and Furth (1986) carried out a study examining rule understanding in profoundly and prelingually deaf children living in residential schools. Their results suggested that deaf children had a less mature understanding of school and societal rules than game rules. They suggested that this may be due to the fact that these children have less opportunity actively to manipulate these rules. Their findings argue powerfully for the role of social experience in the development of social understanding.

While the children's social experiences and understandings are central, the context in which the children find themselves and the wider context in which the special educational needs are managed needs also to be addressed. For example, the nature of the provision needs to be carefully considered. There are social consequences of the type of support that children are offered and the ways in which this support is presented. Where children are placed and how they are provided for may reinforce stigmas or inhibit interactions; alternatively they may improve self-concepts and facilitate learning. Children are keenly aware of differences but how these differences are marked and negotiated can be of major import. Children with special educational needs have different experiences from their peers. These experiences may differ in either amount (e.g. more failure), or kind (e.g. having to wear hearing aids). Children may have difficulties interpreting and assimilating these experiences. The attitudes and beliefs children form as a result of these experiences will influence their developing value system and how they view their wider societal role.

Conclusion

The child's predispositions to organise and categorise the world provides a ready-made basis for the construction of social groups. Yet the values that children develop are not predetermined. Rather, the fledgling value system develops through the experiences children confront, their ability to understand and monitor these experiences and the socio-cultural situations in which they find themselves. The data reviewed here highlight the fact that, as things stand, an understanding of, and a respect for diversity is not transmitted to children through their experiences, or through the conventional education system. It is consistent with a respect for individual variation that children should know and understand about special needs within a context of diversity and respect. Somehow the powerful messages that surround teaching children moral codes conflict with the experiences of many children with special educational needs. Not only does this failure to translate rhetoric into practice devalue the children involved but also it provides a series of contradictory messages for others: contradictory messages which ultimately must be assimilated into a value system.

Developing a value system is a complex endeavour. If we expect children with special needs to be valued in their social situations, we need to consider teaching practices that raise awareness and understanding about diversity and discrimination. This entails a critical analysis of how the value systems we display and accept impact on children's beliefs and their views about themselves as respected members of the community.

Chapter 10

Parental Values and Care for the Child with Special Needs

Roger Attwood and David Thompson

Introduction – Where are the dilemmas?

Education is intended to be a joint responsibility between a child's parents and the community, where each has obligations to support the child's learning. Tensions can occur between parents and the state as they cooperate together for a number of reasons, probably the commonest one being that the state is not providing educational facilities of the type preferred by the parents. When a child has special needs, including special educational needs, parents feel these tensions keenly, because they are very aware of the difficulties their child faces in growing up and learning about the wider world. Parents resent any lost opportunity for their child or any unnecessary difficulty, however mild or severe the problems faced by their child. The more severe the problem, however, the less likely that parents will see mainstream school as the obvious best placement, unless the child is supported effectively in an integrated unit of some kind. Most texts on making provision for children with special needs in mainstream school (see, for example, Ramasut 1989) concentrate on inclusive provision for children with mild or moderate difficulties. A few mainstream schools do deal effectively with more severe difficulties, but it is unlikely that many parents of children with more severe difficulties will find themselves in an appropriate catchment area.

When these tensions over arrangements for education come between people – usually between parents and local educational professionals and administrators – they often have different criteria for judging the acceptability of educational situations for their children. We see the term 'value' as a noun, indicating a stated preference for certain types of aims over other aims, or a verb, to prefer certain conditions over others. In general, educational values give parents and professionals criteria for making judgements about the relative acceptability of aspects of children's education.

Values of parents in practice

Parents see themselves, and are generally seen by the wider community, as being the 'primary carers', and 'the family' as a social unit is generally supported by virtually all social groupings of any description, from local community groups and religious groups to national political parties. Sometimes such support appears only rhetorical, and other values such as 'economic use of resources' or 'trying to stay within budget', may influence the extent to which the rhetoric is implemented. However for the parents the dominance of this value of caring means that they tend to reject events influencing their child when they can see these do not support their child's welfare. Matters such as the availability of finance, the administrative difficulties of pursuing a course of action, or even the psychological difficulties of reconciling their own child's welfare with that of other children do not make undesirable events any more acceptable. The single mindedness which parents can show in pursuit of their own child's welfare can easily be seen by professionals as irrational or not based on any empirical evidence at all, which in turn can lead educationists to seek to minimise the importance of the views and attitudes of parents in the interests of administrative convenience in the education system. Whether such tensions between parental values and the values of the wider community will always exist presumably depends upon the extent to which the wider society insists on parental compliance with social attitudes and legislation, or the extent to which the community supports the welfare of the children, as interpreted by the parents. The debates over how firm the state should be in insisting on infant vaccination, and how generous the state should be in providing the best possible education services are clear examples of these two extremes.

What are the practical expressions of parents' general value of 'caring'? They are expressed in terms such as 'I want the best I can get for my child' which in itself does recognise the impossibility of the ideal in the phrase 'I can get.' In educational terms, this means, at least, an effective education in terms of the basic skills, learning acceptable social behaviour when outside the family, preparation for at least an adequate vocational role through the schooling process, and doing all this in a way which at least the child accepts, if not enjoys. Phrases like 'as long as he is happy' or 'What does he want to do?' are common ways in which parents accept outcomes which they themselves would not have ideally wished for. Parents' knowledge of how far the child's education is being effective in meeting these core parental values is quite detailed, in that they have time to notice just what their child is reading at home, or how well they are getting on socially with their classmates. Their detailed knowledge of the steps towards the achieving of an adequate education gives them a firm base from which to argue with professionals on the adequacy of the education their children are receiving. This general picture is true of all parents. However, when parents find children who have special educational needs in their family, it is more likely that the tensions between their own values of caring and those of the wider community who have the task of providing education for children may be considerably increased.

Tim – a child with very special needs

Tim was eight years old and had complex special educational needs associated with cerebral palsy. There were significant concerns about his self-help and independence skills, physical, social and emotional development, and especially his language and communication skills. In effect he had no speech, though his comprehension, while poor by normal standards, was relatively sound.

He attended a special school where his complex needs were addressed with dedication and considerable skill by a range of professional staff. For instance his class teacher, who coordinated language work throughout the school, introduced him to an ORAC speech synthesiser (the school was a registered ORAC centre). Over time Tim worked his way through increasingly sophisticated arrays of symbols, each of which he had to press to select particular items of recorded speech. His progress both motivated Tim himself, and delighted his parents, who were surprised at his achievements, and revised their expectations of his further progress. Clearly Tim's limits were still to be tested.

Tim's parents were very pleased with his current special school and anticipated no change in his placement. They recognised that the quality of teaching was all important. This was based not just on commitment and sound motivation, but very specialised training and expertise, and, significantly, experience in working over a period with pupils similar to Tim, with all his subtle special educational needs associated with a complex medical condition.

They were aware of support for fully inclusive education, but had little time for this. They felt that those who supported inclusion often did so from a political, philosophical or ideological standpoint, and not necessarily on account of personal involvement in special schooling. Although they knew of some parents with a sincere conviction in favour of inclusion, these seemed to be a vocal minority, who certainly did not represent the views of parents they came into contact with at their son's school. Most of these parents valued special schooling as highly as they did, but did not see the need to express their views publicly, as they took the status quo for granted.

And yet the inclusive movement was beginning to gain ground, if not among those with their particular stake in education, then in the minds of influential people, such as councillors, administrators, educational psychologists and academics. Fewer pupils were being referred for admission to their son's school. The school budget had been cut back sharply in the latest annual settlements. Was this because finance was needed elsewhere to support inclusion initiatives? Was their son's school even viable in the long-term, despite the excellence of its achievements? Would the LEA be drawn to support inclusion not just for reasons of narrow political correctness, but also for reasons of economy? What power did they as parents have to influence wider LEA policy? Was there a covert policy to run down special schools?

They felt that they could do without such uncertainty. Caring for Tim from day to day was quite enough, and left them with little energy or time for campaigning. What they did know was that Tim had only one chance of schooling, and they resented and strongly resisted any suggestion of experimentation with uncertain outcomes.

They knew that the placement was less than ideal in certain respects. One significant disadvantage was that Tim had to travel many miles to and from school daily, along a very busy and potentially hazardous route. Time spent travelling was time wasted, apart from which Tim was tending to become isolated from his home neighbourhood, in a sense even from his brothers, who attended local mainstream schools. His parents could not drop in informally at Tim's school – because of the distance involved every visit required deliberate planning, and no little expense. Furthermore, Tim had to rely mostly on the adults in school for conversation, as few pupils could speak normally. He did attend a nearby mainstream school for half a day a week for 'integration', and got a lot out of this socially. However, this arrangement was not permanent, and depended upon the goodwill of staff and available resourcing. Tim's parents accepted these limitations readily, judging that Tim was attending a fine school in terms of one key measure – the teaching quality.

What could they do to integrate Tim more within his local community? They made an approach to the Cub Pack, where Tim's brother was already a member. The initial response was unfavourable, however. Tim 'failed' a month's trial, and the Cub leaders felt unable to offer him a regular place. Tim's parents met the Cub leaders to discuss their decision. An area representative of the movement argued that as Tim would be unable to do conventional badge work because of his disabilities, there was no point in his membership, in the long run. But was that not concern with the paraphernalia rather than the underlying principles and spirit of the scouting family? Did it not promote helping others? What would Tim's brother make of this message if Tim were excluded from the 'family'. For the first time, faced with a 'No', Tim's parents began to understand the zeal of those who pioneered for inclusion. 'I can't change Tim for you, but you can change for Tim,' said Tim's father, irritated. He had no wish to unsettle the Cub Pack but Tim surely had as much right as any child of his age to join the Cubs, and indeed stood to gain more than most? And what was the alternative to membership? He would just be sitting at home alone, doing nothing in particular. Tim's father argued that just being there would be enough – it was the social contact that mattered, 'progress' on badge work was unimportant. As the discussion proceeded the Cub leaders confided that apprehension and unease over Tim's disabilities was the underlying problem. They simply did not know how to handle him.

A volunteer was found who was at ease with disability, who could interpret and modify Cub activities for Tim, and provide individual support where necessary. From then on it was plain sailing. Other cubs took to Tim very quickly. They did not fuss over him, and were as wild, loud and active as ever. They did not think of him as a problem, but admired him for his determination and positive personality. Tim never felt sorry for himself, and this was quite a lesson for them. The Cub leaders showed imagination in finding legitimate badge awards for Tim, such as a hobbies badge which recognised his regular horse riding with the Riding for Disabled Association, and a community badge for sharing in Cub Pack visits to the fire station and elsewhere. The leaders acknowledged that they learned a lot just by doing, by having Tim around, and found that they had much more to offer him than they had anticipated. Tim had in effect paved the way for the next child with special needs who might wish to join. That child would be accepted with greater confidence. Tim himself wore the uniform proudly and just enjoyed belonging. When he went up on his walking frame to be awarded occasional badges, the cubs gave him an extra clap, and meant it.

Meanwhile the LEA had decided to set up a large-scale review of its special schools. In principle, they argued, all special educational provision should be community based, integrated rather than segregated, and separated out into primary and secondary sectors. What worried his parents was that Tim's special school, despite its fine record and good standing, failed to meet any of these criteria. What did this mean for the future of the school? The suggestion was that local units attached to mainstream school would come to replace special schools. Tim's parents favoured a conservative approach, based upon well established, tried and trusted methods. They would oppose any innovation unless they could see clear advantages for Tim himself. Instead they saw potential difficulties. How could the specialised teaching they so valued in Tim's current school be retained in a unit where the pupil intake would surely be impossibly diverse? Communication therapists and physiotherapists were based in Tim's present school. How much time would they and other specialists spend travelling from unit to unit instead of helping pupils? The local mainstream school was outstandingly good and had sailed through an Ofsted inspection. And yet with existing resources staff were challenged by numbers of pupils with lesser special educational needs than Tim. How then could Tim's needs be met to the standard his parents expected? What about the needs of the majority of pupils already attending there?

Parents would be consulted during the review, but would not be represented on the review body itself. The next challenge was on.

Value conflicts in finding school placements for Tim

The discussions around Tim seem to illustrate some of the central dilemmas for parents very well. Are Tim's parents right to place such strong emphasis on specialist teaching quality, and to assume that this can only be developed and maintained in a specialised setting? Are they right to place a lesser value on the social context of Tim's schooling? Are educationists holding inclusive views of education right to hold them when they are dealing with a child with as many special needs as Tim, where delivering effective education in mainstream would mean completely unrealistic resourcing and staffing? Such views place the importance of providing education in as normal a context as possible as the first priority, and then assuming or hoping that the actual curriculum content and other provision would be developed as a result of that inclusion process.

In Tim's case, at the beginning of the story his specialised needs for a highly structured curriculum and teaching methods were being met through segregated education but also at least some of his needs for contact with the peer group around him were also being met by his inclusion in the Cub movement. Are educationists right therefore to assume that schools must meet all the needs of each child? Could not school meet some of his needs, leaving the parents and the wider community to meet other sets of needs? Presumably if this approach is taken the set of needs which should be met by state provision is that set which is most difficult for the parents and the community to provide independently – in this case, highly specialised teaching.

Looking at Tim's situation, which illustrates the particularity of individual need, it is clear that from the local authority's perspective a mixed model of provision is a great strength. If a range of provision is available, then every case can be treated on its individual needs and merits. One difficulty comes of course with the expense of maintaining specialist provision. There is always a finite limit to budgets. Another difficulty comes with the very intensity of the commitment to inclusion and normalisation by LEAs, both politicians and officers. The greater that commitment, the more the available budget will be spent in supporting the mainstream situation, and the more likely it is that the benefits of specialised teaching staff, curricula and teaching methods will be dissipated – as each mainstream setting will only be supporting a handful of children with specialised needs, at most, and so will be unlikely to develop the breadth and depth of specialised knowledge potentially available in a more specialised situation. This core dilemma is well illustrated by Jack's situation, below, and two parts of his story.

Jack – moving to college

Jack had Severe Learning Difficulties and was physically disabled. He attended a special school where pupils were expected to leave at 16 years of age. As he was already 15 the head teacher prompted consideration of post-school opportunities. He invited Jack's parents into school to meet the teacher with special responsibility for school leavers, who gave them a lot of information on courses for 16–19 year olds in various FE colleges within the county, and further afield. During a lengthy discussion it emerged that the school favoured one particular option, based upon their close knowledge of Jack over several years and their assessment of his physical and intellectual capabilities, emotional maturity, personality and interests. In fact they had already introduced him to the residential college in question, on a social visit which he had enjoyed. Jack's parents knew this because several times following the visit Jack had said a word which sounded like 'college', each time with a laugh and a smile on his face. He had also gestured 'sleep' in Makaton, indicating clearly enough to his parents that he appreciated the possibility of residence there, and regarded this as a positive, grown-up prospect.

Jack's parents arranged to view the college for themselves, taking Jack along with them. They were aware of the college's sound reputation, but had open minds on placement, conscious of the distance away from home for a young man who would remain highly dependent and vulnerable, and was very young for his years. They had some apprehension over residence for a possible three years. Would he return home a different person, having grown away from them?

On arrival their immediate impression was favourable. They noticed that the premises were in good order, and the grounds immaculately maintained. The atmosphere was both business-like and welcoming. They were met by a senior member of staff who escorted them around. The college had one very clear central purpose: to prepare students realistically for adulthood, giving them as much personal independence, choice and control over their lives as possible. The college had been working on this theme for a generation, specialising in students with significant disabilities. The staff were experienced enough to be confident and positive-minded, they knew that they made a real difference and were committed to achieving this.

What was implicit in the college's approach was that the students' futures mattered, that they had the same human value as any others, and were to be accorded dignity and respect. This was a matter of key importance to Jack's parents and a tour of the college added to their confidence. There were high quality special facilities for IT, drama, art and domestic science, and these were being developed continuously. Residential accommodation was personalised, offered some privacy, and some of the bedrooms overlooked the beautiful landscaped gardens. The art work on display in the corridors explored themes of self-awareness, identity and individuality, as did drama sessions. Pop music of the students' own choice was being played in the dining hall, and there was talk of trips out on the town to concerts as for any students of their age. Bathrooms and kitchens used in college were in some cases designed to match those which the students would have to cope with in their subsequent adult accommodation.

The member of staff pushed Jack around in his wheelchair, quickly establishing a rapport. He was unfazed by Jack's poor speech and addressed questions to him directly, rather than through his parents, who were so accustomed to speaking on Jack's behalf. The parents felt uncomfortable at first in stepping back, but took the point that it was Jack's own views and interests which counted now, not their interpretation. Already Jack was being set new expectations, being offered greater independence.

By the end of the visit the member of staff had conducted his own informal assessment. Jack was in the middle range of students admitted to the college, in terms of physical disabilities and intellectual level. This meant that the college was likely to have encountered previously any particular challenges and difficulties Jack himself might present. They would be able to cope. This would scarcely be the case in mainstream FE colleges nearer home, where Jack would present tremendous challenges, and where his special needs would be considered extreme and exceptional, compared to other students.

Jack's parents felt encouraged and reassured by their visit. Here was a placement of quality to aim for, an opportunity which would help them to plan for Jack's future, at least for the next few years.

'Caring' values in the placement

The college provided a near ideal reflection of some of the values which the parents held dear.

The college was clearly committed to its own long-term purposes of providing effective support for the young people, and had the necessary skilled staff with well developed specialist experience to be confident in meeting its aims. In particular, it was committed to helping the young people develop their vocational and independence skills, with realistic and detailed assessment procedures, and careful preparation for future training, college and adult placements.

The college also saw its role in supporting youngsters in their emotional and ethical development, through the relationships the college and its staff constructed with students and its emphasis on providing choices for the emerging individuals. This meant offering high quality accommodation to boost self-identity, keeping the young people out of emotional dependency on parents, and respecting their choices and decisions.

This case study raises a number of questions. How can professionals and other establishments emulate such interventions? Is it easier to provide education in a highly specialised setting? Is it easier to provide this appropriately at the 16–19 year level? Do mainstream colleges struggle because their SEN courses are under-developed or are there inherent difficulties associated with an all-abilities student intake?

The case study also reflects the issue of the parents' actual power and influence. The parents may consider the placement excellent. This does not guarantee a place for Jack. What influence should parents have? Do caring responsibilities confer on parents any additional rights? What power should they have to maintain their family links with their child and claim an appropriate placement?

Jack's review meeting

Some time later, Jack's parents attended a statutory Social Service Department review meeting. They tended not to enjoy such meetings, expecting to find them tiring and trying. They felt out on a limb from others present – after all they were the only ones not being paid to be there, and they felt uncomfortably beholden to professional staff for services provided rather than feeling entitled to them. Most of all, they alone had a powerful emotional link to Jack, and an unreserved lifetime's commitment. It was their child who was the focus of discussion, and if they felt tense it was because they did not have the comfort of professional detachment. Even seeing his name in print was a trial to them as it set him apart from ordinary children.

Some staff were well aware of these issues, and made a point of drawing parents into proceedings, realising that they had a unique viewpoint and a valuable contribution to offer. The tone of the meetings was always set by the chair, the service manager. Unfortunately today's manager was the third different one in successive review meetings. He had never met Jack and was never likely to. As Jack's parents saw it, the meeting was conducted in a curiously stilted, legalistic manner, as if meeting statutory requirements was the main point. There was no time for informal discussion which might have put Jack's parents more at ease. Why the formality? Was it pressure of time, or lack of practical experience of special needs issues in the manager's part? Or did it reflect the new manager's need to establish his authority?

In this orderly atmosphere the parents were expected to outline Jack's disabilities for the benefit of the manager. This was something they had done countless times before to people who came and went in Jack's life, and something they hated doing. It was distressing, it became no easier with repetition, and seemed to them an invasion of privacy.

A written account of the meeting arrived through the post a while later. It was misleading and inaccurate in many details and betrayed a lack of familiarity with Jack and his parents as clients. The actual services Jack and his family received – the respite care, the programme of holiday and leisure time activities – were excellent. The field level social workers had given Jack exciting and adventurous experiences against the odds, considering his disabilities: they had given him some times to remember. To Jack's parents it seemed that an opportunity had been missed to celebrate this, and place it on record. Jack's father wrote corrections on the report, intending to return it. But what was the point? By now the manager had already moved on to another post. Maybe Jack's father could comment more assertively at the next review. What bothered him was that in a period of threatened cuts to services, fieldwork activities of real value which were not acknowledged might disappear.

This kind of case review meeting will appear as a reasonably typical one for many professionals, but expresses many of parents' concerns and illustrates how the support system can challenge parental values. Continuity in bureaucratic procedures is so important for the parents, and the feeling that professionals appreciate the emotional dimensions of parents can be the first casualty in budget reductions affecting fieldwork services. When parents have such reactions, they feel how fragile good care and education of their children is, and their marginalised position is re-emphasised – again (Osborne 1994).

What is the point of review meetings involving parents? Is it a genuine involvement in care planning, or a demonstration that the minimum statutory requirements are being made by the local authority?

What distinguishes parents of children with special educational needs?

In general, there are five major differences identifiable between parents of children with special needs and parents of children without such needs. Some of these differences are a question of degree rather than a categorical difference. They are long-term players, in that they know that their children will be dependent on them for many things for a much longer period than would be the case if their children had no special needs (Hewett 1970). Secondly, they have a tendency to become slightly isolated from other parents, as their own children's needs and the stages that their children go through diverge from those of other families. Thirdly, they are more concerned for their own children rather than any other groups that their children may be members of, such as classes in mainstream school, as they know that their own children's needs are likely to be different from those of the groups. Fourthly, the natural emotional involvement of parents with children is heightened, in view of the constant knowledge that failure and marginalisation is a much more constant threat for their own children than for others. Finally, they know that the long-term welfare of their children is much more dependent on the continued effectiveness of the family as a social unit providing care and support than with other families, who can look towards the increasing independence of their children from the family unit itself. Parents' activities and attitudes have to maintain the integrity of the nuclear family unit as a major priority, as this is the unit that their children will be dependent on into the foreseeable future.

Parents as long-term players

Their commitment to their children's welfare may involve loss of career opportunities, earnings, pension rights, prestige, as well as a wide range of social contacts. Society expects parents to take indefinite responsibility for the care of their disabled children, and recent legislation has further strengthened parental responsibilities – emotional, physical and financial. Parents themselves may easily feel that this responsibility extends beyond the parents' own death – and they are often interested in making what provision they can for the quality of life of their children in years to come (Hewett 1970).

Parents look for the 'enduring' values of continuity and consistency of care, and the general dependability of the caring structure will be reflected in the kind of provision made. This means that the parents will tend to value well established educational provisions, specialist experience and expertise, teaching styles which they see as being tried and tested and, in general, approaches which emphasise the long-term benefits to the clients in helping them develop practical and relevant skills for living.

This interest in the continuity and consistency of care also reflects parents' expectations that their children are more likely to be more dependent for a longer period of time on the care provided by the adults in the community and the caring agencies. Parents of non-disabled children can expect them to grow to independence at the usual speed, so that by the time they are 18–20 years old they are certainly capable of earning their own living and providing emotional security for themselves from their own peer group. This progression to independence will be much slower for disabled children, and for an appreciable minority may in fact never occur. Parents' interests in continuity of care are based on very real situations.

Questions arise at this point about how well prepared local education authorities are to provide for such values as consistency, continuity and specialist help over the long term. The general speed of educational change affects institutions drastically, and in addition individual professional advancement may well depend on gaining experience in a number of relevant fields and moving jobs frequently. Such pressures inevitably have a tendency to disrupt the very continuity of care which parents value.

Tendency to isolation

The caring imperative on parents means that a reduced lifestyle may be taken for granted. Particularly with the more severe special educational needs, many restrictions appear on family activities and even such simple activities as going to the shops, going on family day trips, and playing out in the neighbourhood may be restricted, apart from the problems of going on longer holidays. Access to community facilities including local schools may be blocked, resulting in a loss of the 'normal' choices available to parents. Even within the separate special educational provision, parents choice may be minimal or non-existent. They find themselves adopting different goals for their children from those of other parents. Rather than thinking of advancing through the usual key stages and getting into the school football teams, parents of children with special needs find themselves concentrating on helping their children walk, talk, feed themselves and achieve effective toilet training long after these have been mastered by most families. This tendency for parents of children with special needs to see themselves as more isolated than other families even tends to be reinforced by the statutory approaches, as legislation in general tends to be drafted with the needs of the majority in mind.

The effects of this may be dis-empowering and marginalising for the parents concerned. This gives an onus on the local education authority not to push this marginalisation even further, for example by having administrative procedures which are impersonal or distant. This particularly applies in the operation of the special needs assessment procedures, when there are great differences in how the procedures operate from one local authority to another. Even within similar procedural structures, there are still differences in how openly decisions about provision for individuals and for groups are made. Annual reviews of children's progress may be experienced very differently by parents, even if the apparent bureaucratic procedures are standard. This raises the whole issue of the nature of partnership with parents. Expectations can be easily raised by optimistic sounding legislation, even if the small print in fact minimises parental power to actually change local education authority decisions. Sometimes parents who feel themselves marginalised and often ignored can react by seeking real power, including the ability to determine acceptable provision for their children from their own priorities rather than accepting professional views on how adequate any given provision is.

In these arenas, the crucial element is often not the formal LEA structures but the values shown by the professionals operating those structures. The professionals in particular often find themselves in conflicting situations, an obvious one being where their genuine desire to communicate as openly as possible with parents and take their priorities seriously is in conflict with their desire to work towards a smooth continuation of a pattern of provision in circumstances of reduced budgets. Similarly, 'confidentiality' (which was originally introduced to protect the interests of families) may easily be interpreted in a way which minimises effective information transfer. Possibly the key question to be answered in instances such as this is, 'Whose interests are being served by withholding information?'

Concern for their own children rather than for groups

Parents are well aware that local education authorities have to consider groups of children in establishing provision, and also in allocating children to it. However, their own child has to be the centre of the universe. Issues such as, 'What are the available resources?' can become a resented background to parental striving to ensure that their own child's needs are met as fully as possible.

The rights of individual children to have their needs met has been supported by recent legislation, and the regulations stemming from it. The Code of Practice for the assessment of special educational needs in schools

(Department for Education 1994) and the arrangements for appeals tribunals are both built on the notion of individual pupils' needs being met. It is perhaps inevitable that clashes will occur as LEAs must consider numbers of children in their area with similar special needs, and they must have some notion of equity in level of provision between those children. Different sets of parents may also have different priorities for forms of provision, depending on their individual child's particular needs, and it is even possible that parents of children of the same age and having the same general needs may differ on their emphasis. For example the extent to which caring includes pushing for independence for their children differs from one set of parents to another. Independence always involves taking some degree of risks of failure, and parents respond differently to this dilemma.

Emotional involvement

The intense emotional involvement of parents arises from the fact that their responsibility as parents has no limits. The responsibilities are not usually taken up out of choice, and there are no set hours for which they can be adopted. Where the special needs make children more vulnerable, for example if the child was premature, or delicate or chronically ill, then the child's safety, comforts, and contentment are likely to be a high priority for parents. This intensity of emotional involvement may also restrict their levels of acceptance of the extent of their child's special needs, or affect their extent of understanding of its implications. The high level of emotional involvement can make parents ready to believe claims made for treatments which apparently offer 'solutions' – such as the quasi-medical approaches of conductive education, particular drug treatment and other approaches advocated by high profile and convincing professionals on the basis of marginal or disputed evidence. Parents' commitment to such approaches may well seem irrational to other professionals, who are much more aware of limitations of treatment regimes.

The welfare of the family as a unit

Parents also value activities which support all members of the family. They are aware of the needs of any other children they may have, and indeed of their own needs for time, space and emotional support. This can act in an opposing way to emotional involvement with the individual disabled child and the concern for their own child rather than for groups, but the parents' broader knowledge of the way their own family functions can be crucial in acting so as to maintain the mental health of the family at large and to continue the level of care for the child with difficulties.

Values underlying the decisions of LEA officers

Clearly, all officers whether administrative or professional, would like well resourced provision. At any given level of resourcing, however, particularly at the lower levels where there is clearly not enough money to pay for services to meet needs, they will have certain underlying general principles which they will try to use in coming to decisions. Such values may include the normalisation of children with special needs as far as possible, and their inclusion in mainstream settings. Officers will also tend to value the mechanisms that they know are in place to support such inclusion, such as the support teacher services, and mechanisms for individual resourcing with the statements of special educational needs. They will also value achieving a shared consensus between the parents and themselves, as enabling action to be taken in a way which includes the parents' priorities. From the parents' point of view however achieving this consensus might involve their accepting so many qualifications to their own original priorities for provision that achieving a consensus amounts to compulsion to accept the LEA officers' views.

Two values held by local authority staffs are probably emphasised by the institutional roles they have: the belief that the mechanisms that the LEA has in place to support integration do work effectively, and the value given to achieving a shared consensus among the parties to a decision. These are clearly principles they have to believe in order to continue operating in the LEA structure. Similarly, the long-term values of consistency and access to specialised services held by parents are an inescapable part of their role as parents.

Resolution of value conflicts

Value conflicts can usually only be resolved in specific instances, where real priorities can be reached based on real events. The two studies of Tim and Jack have illustrated the typical details which play a large part in working towards the resolution of value conflicts. The meetings between parents, teachers and administrators are the arenas for resolution of value conflicts – but such resolutions will only occur when all participants trust each other to have the same commitment to high quality effective educational arrangements appropriate to a commonly held view of the child's needs, and if all parties put a high value on reaching a true consensus (McConkey 1985). In a very real sense, if this happens all participants are forming a specific personal partnership to meet the child's needs effectively in a way which accepts the five parental characteristics outlined above. This partnership then can find itself using common values – common ways of judging the effectiveness of education. Parent partnership schemes initiated by some LEAs in recent years (Furze and Conrad 1997) have attempted to provide some staffing and other resources to support development of partnerships, but doubts remain as to their ultimate effectiveness in a market-driven national education system where resources are limited (Armstrong 1995). Partnerships do, in addition, go wider than between parents and the LEA officers – Social Services departments are often heavily involved in provision, as they were in Jack's case – and there needs to be thought and commitment on the part of the national service providers about to how to coordinate their services effectively to include parents as full partners (Dessent 1996).

Values and political relationships

In practice, of course, professionals are employed by the LEA to operate a given system of assessment and provision, and may not be free to join in partnership with parents in the true sense (Wilding 1982). Insofar as this limits partnership, the question then becomes one of the political relationships between the two groups – parents and children on the one hand and professionals and LEAs on the other. The debate then moves from the communicating and sharing of views and values into rights and statutory responsibilities. This may be regrettable, but it is sometimes inevitable, as there clearly is a conflict of interest between the two sides resulting from meeting the child's needs within organisational and budgetary constraints (Simmons 1996). The political process will be working towards setting up the administrative framework to be as helpful as possible, but due to the diversity of needs among families and children, the gap, and the tensions, will always ultimately be there. The aim for the professionals must be to work towards the partnership – and in some instances where the LEA has been able to plan flexible provision, partnership will be possible for some children and their parents.

Chapter 11

Translating Values into Rights: Respecting the Voice of the Child

Robert Burden

So what's the problem?

It has always seemed to me to be an interesting paradox that those of us working within the educational system who are particularly committed to helping children identified as falling somehow outside 'the norm', can find ourselves acting in ways which we know in our heart of hearts are not in those children's best interests. As an educational psychologist working for a fairly enlightened LEA in the 1960s, for example, I found myself recommending the placement of children in special schools on the basis of what I came to believe to be inappropriate psychometric test scores which, at their best, provided information on a limited range of educational skills and abilities. Often I had very little knowledge of the schools to which I was recommending that the children be transferred and sometimes the knowledge that I did have gave me justifiable cause for concern.

But, as these schools and institutions carried the imprimatur of 'special', I found myself assuming without question that they were the right place for children designated as suffering from one or another category of educational 'handicap'. Rarely, if ever, were the children's wishes or concerns taken into account. It was always assumed that if we professionals could persuade the parents that we were acting in their child's best interests, then it must be so. Even more rarely did we carry out any kind of ongoing or follow-up evaluation studies to assess whether our assumptions had been correct or even justifiable.

I cannot help wondering, with the benefit of hindsight, whether some of the horror stories that have emerged over the past 20 years about the systematic abuse of children placed 'in care' or residential special schools were an indirect result of some of our arrogant assumptions about how best to meet the needs of troubled and disturbing children. Such assumptions, it seems to me, were often made on the basis of limited and limiting information and, just as importantly, without a thorough analysis of the philosophical premises upon which they were based. As Bolton (1990) has pointed out, psychology cannot stand alone as a discipline and needs to be applied in conjunction with its sister disciplines of philosophy and sociology if it is to make a worthwhile contribution to society.

Since that time there have been profound changes in attitude towards the most appropriate forms of education for children with special educational needs, not least by virtue of the introduction of the term 'need' itself via the Warnock Report (Department of Education and Science 1978) and the 1981 Education Act. At the same time, philosophical and sociological analyses of the assumptions underlying segregated educational provision (e.g. Tomlinson 1982) have highlighted the logical flaws and potentially damaging effects of such assumptions. In particular, the rights of children to be offered equal educational opportunities were identified as being seriously at risk.

In recent years the contentious issue of children's rights has been brought to the forefront of the public consciousness by the activities of the Children's Legal Centre (e.g. Rosenbaum and Newell 1991), such media promoted activities as *Children in Need* and *Childline*, the 1989 Children Act, the World Summit for Children held in 1990 and, perhaps most spectacularly, the 1989 United Nations Convention on the Rights of the Child (John 1994; Lansdown 1994). The issue is contentious because it is clear from the current media-inspired debate on returning corporal punishment to state schools and the never-ending debate on parents' rights to smack (or even beat) their offspring that a significant proportion of the adult population do not consider that children should have rights, let alone that these should be respected.

One of the most distressing aspects of many reported cases of child abuse in its various forms is that no one seemed to listen to, let alone hear, the voices of the victims however long and loud they cried. It would appear that, even amongst the most well-meaning teachers, psychologists and care-workers, a conspiracy of deafness can exist with regard to the right of children to be heard. This can occur at every level, not just in extreme cases of abuse, and in itself it is illustrative of an entrenched view of the position of children within our society whereby they are afforded few rights and almost no power.

It is the purpose of this chapter to explore some of the ways in which the rights of children have been ignored or overlooked by those allegedly working on their behalf and show how such apparent indifference to what may seem relatively less important issues can reveal a huge discrepancy between what Donald Schön describes as our *espoused theories* – what we say we believe – and our *theories in action* – what our actions reveal we really believe – (Schön 1983). The chapter will focus on one particular aspect of children's rights, that of *participation,* and will suggest ways in which this can be increased in accordance with the kind of values perspective that runs through this book.

The challenge to educational psychology

It could be argued that the history of applied educational (school) psychology has been one of power relationships within which groups of powerful people (educational psychologists, teachers, administrators) have acted in a variety of different ways towards or on behalf of a virtually powerless group (children). These powerful groups have selected the ground, the topic, the methods and the outcomes while the powerless group has been forced to play the role of the passive recipient, albeit for what are articulated as the best possible reasons.

Nowhere is this more evident than in the field of assessment, where educational psychologists currently find themselves performing an essentially classificatory function despite the rhetoric of the 1981 Education Act with its superficial emphasis upon the identification of educational needs, or even the apparently enlightened approach offered by the 1994 Code of Practice (Department for Education 1994).

Assessment, as is well known to almost anyone outside of the political arena, means more than simply 'testing'. It also has a wide range of possible functions beyond categorisation – the assessment of skills, attitudes, interest and intentions, to name but a few. It does not necessarily imply a passive role for the person being assessed. Nevertheless, until recently, with one or two honourable exceptions (Ravenette 1980; Gersch 1992) references in the professional literature to the involvement of children in their own assessment procedures have been virtually non-existent.

A paper by Ronald Davie (1993), first delivered in October 1991 to the Education Section of the British Psychological Society as their Vernon-Wall lecture, highlighted the revolutionary nature of the Butler-Sloss Enquiry's recommendations, later cushioned in the 1989 Children Act, that professionals should always listen carefully to what the child has to say and to take seriously what is said. Moreover, the court order known as the Child Assessment Order which may call for a child to be assessed also contains the rider *'that the child may, if he is of sufficient understanding to make an informed decision, refuse to submit to the examination or other assessment'*. Although this raises the tricky question of what exactly constitutes 'sufficient understanding' and is essentially framed as the right to say 'no', it also places the onus on the prospective assessor to convince children that such assessments will be in their best interests.

If all of us who are involved in contributing to formal assessment procedures were to take such a responsibility seriously, we would find ourselves faced once again with many of the issues arising from the application of our value systems that have been raised previously in this book. As has been pointed out elsewhere (Horton 1990), there are at least five different and often conflicting functions of formal assessment. The emphasis that is given to any one of these functions will reflect, at least in part, the underlying philosophical and ethical foundations of those carrying out the assessment. It is exactly the conflicting demands of these different assessment functions that can lead to a schizoid reaction within many educational psychologists by bringing into sharp focus the question of 'who is my primary client?'

The implications of taking a human rights perspective

The International School Psychology Association (ISPA) has attempted to face up to such issues by emphasising in its constitution its commitment to the furtherance of children's rights (Burden 1992).

At its most basic level this requires school psychologists to stop sitting on the fence and 'come out' as child advocates. The message is, however, ultimately more complex and profound in that it presents the challenge to psychologists of finding ways of helping children to speak and act on their own behalf. This in turn presupposes that they are capable of doing so in a reasonable and reasoning (as well as passionate) manner and that psychology has something special to offer in this respect. In recent years ISPA has been considerably helped in this endeavour by the introduction of the United Nations Convention on the Rights of the Child. This landmark document was adopted by the UN in 1989 and ratified by 147 nations in 1993. It provides 54 articles which aim to provide a comprehensive definition of the whole range of children's rights and to enshrine these in international law.

Although the United Nations convention on the Rights of the Child was passed unanimously by the UN General Assembly in November 1989, it was not ratified in the United Kingdom until a good two years later – and then with the proviso that not all of the 54 articles were acceptable. This is not in itself surprising as some of the Articles, such as the right of children to bear arms, are highly contentious. What is surprising is the fact that the Convention itself received such a powerful measure of support from over 150 countries in an extraordinarily brief length of time.

Excellent summaries of the convention and some of its most important implications have been provided elsewhere (John 1994) and it is not the purpose of this chapter to repeat that process. However, John and others have helpfully pointed out that the Articles of the Convention can be conveniently grouped under four headings: *prevention*, which mainly covers health related issues; *provision*, which covers such issues as equal access to education and the rights of disabled children to share in the their communities; *protection*, from abduction, neglect, abuse, and exploitation; and *participation*, which emphasises the right of all children to express their views on matters and have them taken seriously. All of these are important but it is the contention of this chapter that the issue of participation is the one to which psychology has the most to offer.

What is sometimes not fully understood is that once a nation has ratified the UN Convention, it has a responsibility to implement at the very least those clauses that are deemed acceptable. In this way the issue of adopting a human rights perspective in our work with children moves from an abstract ideal to an essential condition. The central question related to children's participation then becomes not 'Should we seek to involve children in decisions that affect them?' but 'How can we best accomplish this?' The role of the psychologist thereby becomes one of advocate and active supporter of children's empowerment.

One educational psychologist who has written very persuasively for a number of years about ways of involving pupils in their own assessments and of empowering them to represent their individual viewpoints has been Irvine Gersch (e.g. Gersch 1992; Gersch *et al.* 1993). Gersch and his colleagues have been instrumental in introducing a high degree of pupil involvement in one London borough by means of pupil and student reports, surveys of pupil perceptions of various aspects of their schools and schooling, and by action research projects designed to increase professional advocacy for children and to encourage the children themselves to take greater responsibility for their own actions.

Gersch (1996) makes the helpful point that pupil involvement can be more helpfully regarded in terms of a continuum rather than as an absolute concept. He also provides a balanced perspective on the recent tendency to regard children's views as extremely reliable when it is clear that such a view is sometimes unrealistic. Thus it is important to take a realistic stance in recognising children as minors who need a carefully trained listening ear together with guidance and support. It is here that we face one of the dilemmas of the children's rights approach – the clash that can sometimes occur between the right to protection and the right to participation. It is not entirely unknown for some writers to promote arrant nonsense in claiming that children should be afforded the same participatory rights as any adult.

Nevertheless, there is a multitude of ways in which children can be encouraged to become more participatory in decision making about their future welfare and education, as is emphasised in the 1994 Code of Practice on the Identification and Assessment of Special Educational Needs. Here it is explicitly stated that:

> schools should make every effort to identify the ascertainable views and wishes of the child or young person about his or her current and future education ... Schools should, for example, discuss the purpose of a particular assessment arrangement with the child; invite comments from the child, and consider the use of pupil reports and systematic feedback to the child concerned. (DfE 1994, pp.14–15)

An increasing number of descriptions of attempts to empower children by taking a human rights perspective have been published in the UK in recent years. Jones and Marchant (1993), for example, describe the establishment of a Charter of Rights at Chailey Heritage Centre for children with complex physical and multiple disabilities by means of a child protection working group. In an attempt to combat the sense of worthlessness felt by many of the children attending the Centre, the working group emphasised their rights to be valued as individuals, to be treated with dignity and respect, to be loved and cared for as a child first and to be safe. Here we see an example of the protection aspect of rights, but it is also noteworthy that no mention is made by the authors of whether the children themselves were involved in the discussions leading to the establishment of the Charter on their behalf or whether greater participation resulted from it.

In carrying out their assessment role educational psychologists can do things to children, can do things *for* children, or can do things *with* children. Most commonly they perform the first of these functions, which they are quite likely to justify in terms of the second. They are far less likely to perform the third function, within which the children's participatory rights are paramount. If we are to take the notion of children's rights seriously, this participatory function must be our starting point.

Starting from a human rights perspective leads to the following minimal requirements for any assessment process involving two or more people – the assessor(s) and the assessee(s).

Any person subjected to a formal assessment process should be afforded the right to:

• know that such a decision has been made
• know why that decision has been made
• question that decision, should they feel so inclined
• refuse to participate if they feel that it is not in their best interests to do so
• be fully informed about how that assessment will be carried out
• question the validity of the assessment process at any point during that process
• contribute personally to the assessment process in any way possible and practicable
• be fully informed of the outcome of the assessment, of how it will be arrived at and interpreted
• dispute the efficacy of any decisions if they consider them to be against their best interest.

There are no strong reasons to believe that such conditions should not apply to children as well as adults provided, as the Children Act states, that they are of sufficient understanding to make an informed decision. But what does this notion of informed decision making actually involve? Franklin (1995) makes a distinction between what he terms *welfare* rights (e.g. to education, health, etc.) which require the protection or promotion of the holder's interests, and *liberty* rights, most notably to participate in decision making. The problem with the latter is that they require the holders to be capable of making and exercising choices. The key question with which we are faced here is not so much when, chronologically, children are capable of making such choices, but how they can best be helped to do so.

The two main arguments against affording children participating rights are that they are not capable of making rational and informed decisions, and that their very lack of experience makes them prone to mistakes. There is, of course, a case to be made for both these points of view. However, as Franklin (1995) points out, there is considerable evidence that children are capable of making sophisticated and complex choices when required to do so. Moreover, if they are never given the opportunity of making choices which affect their own lives, when will they ever learn to do so? The fact that they may make mistakes is not reason enough to deny them the opportunity since adults are constantly making huge mistakes and appearing not to learn from them.

A stronger case can be made for the need for 'caretakers' to make decisions in children's best interests in order to guarantee their future independence e.g. by choosing an appropriate form of education for them and insisting that they attend school even though they might not want to. As Dworkin (1977) makes clear, here the emphasis is upon what the child will come to welcome rather than on what he or she currently welcomes. In Archard's terms, the caretaker 'chooses for the child in the person of the adult which the child is not yet but will eventually be' (Archard 1993 p.53).

Hart (1992) has offered the metaphor of an eight runged ladder as a means of describing the steps that can be taken to move from paternalism to participation by children in the decision making process, although he also points out that his rungs should not be seen as incremental or sequential stages which must be passed through in any kind of order. The first three rungs can be seen as representing *involvement* rather than true participation. These include: *manipulation*, where children may be consulted but never given any feedback; *decoration*, where their decorative nature is used e.g. for singing or dancing at conferences; and *tokenism*, where 'representative' children may be involved who do not truly represent the views of the group to which they are alleged to belong.

Above this lower level of involvement there are five rungs of genuine, graded participation. The first is where children are *assigned but informed*, i.e. where adults make the important decisions but participating children are well informed about their assigned role and can perform this meaningfully. Subsequent rungs of the ladder include: *consulted and informed; adult designed with shared decisions with children; child designed and directed; and child designed with shared decisions with adults*. Interestingly, this approach mirrors that of Meighan who in another context refers to different conceptions that teachers have of learners, ranging from learners as resisters or as clay to be moulded, through to learners as independent and democratic explorers (Meighan, 1990).

Wider aspects of participating empowerment

There are now demands within a number of different important documents for children to be afforded the right to express their own views on matters pertaining to their education and welfare – the 1989 Children Act, the 1994 Code of Practice and, most significantly, the 1989 United Nations Convention on the Rights of the Child. Article 12 of the UN Convention specifically states that:

> States Parties shall assure to the child who is capable of forming his or her own views the right to express those views freely in all matters affecting the child, the views of the child being given due weight in accordance with the age and maturity of the child.

The establishment of student councils is one way in which some schools have tried to live out this principle, but the danger of this becoming a superficial smokescreen for further covert power wielding by manipulative teachers should not be dismissed too lightly.

At a time when the media is full of stories of increasing disruptive behaviour in schools coupled with violence against teachers, there follows the inevitable strident outcry for firmer discipline and harsher sanctions 'to restore order'. The subtext beneath such demands reflects once again the powerlessness of children. Few ask for the pupils' opinions about the situation in schools, but the outcry instead is for a return to corporal punishment to restore the ancient virtues. Even powerful teachers' unions lay the blame for the ills of the British education system on 'unteachable' pupils. What is conveniently forgotten is that a government enquiry leading to the publication of a sensible and constructive report (Department for Education and Science 1989) discovered little evidence for a breakdown in discipline and provided a number of helpful suggestions about how to encourage positive school discipline policies. One of the most effective methods by far is to involve all of the pupils in the school in drawing up a 'whole school' behaviour policy. If pupils' opinions are sought and genuinely listened to in such matters, what is likely to emerge will almost always be sensible, positive and comprehensively beneficial. In simple terms, pupils tend not to break rules that they themselves have helped to set. If they do break the rules, they are far more likely also to accept any sanctions that they themselves have imposed without resentfully falling back on the age-old excuse of, 'It's not fair!'

Discipline is not the same as punishment or even control. Self-discipline and concern for the needs and rights of others come from having one's own rights acknowledged and respected. However, this does not mean that the allocation of rights or the responsible application of them by individuals thus empowered is a simple and straightforward task. Far from it. In an important paper entitled '*Intergenerational Conflict of Rights: Cultural Imposition and Self-Realisation*', Feuerstein and Hoffman (1982) drew a fundamental distinction between *the right to be* and the *right to become*. Although these can often be in conflict with one another, the authors argue that this need not necessarily be the case and that a complementary balance should be sought. Affording rights to children does not and should not mean allowing them complete freedom to act as they please. There is a responsibility on the part of the adults who care for them to *mediate* appropriate ways of thinking and acting in order to enable them to develop in ways that lead to true self-actualisation and constructive contributions to the betterment of society.

For Feuerstein, as for many others one answer lies in teaching children to learn how to learn and to think critically about important issues that affect them and the societies in which they live. In arriving at her own understanding of her growing interest in thinking skills programmes, Parfitt (1996) found herself reflecting on the question 'How could young people be advocates for themselves if they did not know how to argue about things that mattered to them?' Parfitt describes her efforts to evaluate the introduction of thinking skills into one comprehensive school's curriculum. There have been many such attempts but what makes Parfitt's account interestingly different from most is the links that she makes with enabling the participating pupils to engage in a much more informed dialogue about rights issues.

The teaching of thinking skills as a separate curriculum subject is itself highly contentious and there are many who consider that the issue of citizenship should play a prominent part at the heart of the school curriculum. There are also those who argue that the issue goes even wider and deeper than this. In the words of Abdullah-Pretceille: 'Educating people in human rights means trying to train them on both the individual and social plane. It is not, therefore, any neutral or ordinary process, but a campaign' (1989 p.63).

In an impressive paper on educating children about human rights at the pre-school level, Abdullah-Pretceille indicates two possible routes, the *prescriptive*, whereby values are imposed, as say from a religious perspective, and compliance is demanded, in contrast to what might be termed the *socially constructed*, within which the child has a role as both actor and subject. The latter viewpoint actively opposes the reduction of human rights to any moral code, even of a secular nature.

The social constructivist perspective on human rights teaching is closely related to the humanist approach of Carl Rogers. It places great emphasis upon education as an active process rather than one in which knowledge is transmitted from powerful, all-knowing adults to passively receptive pupils. It also emphasises the need for teachers to give as much consideration to what they are and what they do as to what they say. This is not to argue that that this form of education is indicative of some form of 'soft' post-modern relativism. Again, in the words of Abdullah-Pretceille: 'Education in human rights ... is a matter of deliberate choice and is unable to accommodate any "perhapses" or "maybes". Each system must declare its options and everyone must stand by their commitments.' (1989 p.66)

A further point of importance here is the need to create conditions in schools to ensure that human rights are respected long before a specific type of education is introduced. This should help us to see the weaknesses in much of the rhetoric about 'inclusion' and 'mainstreaming'. It is not enough merely to place all children of whatever race, creed or disability in 'inclusive' schools, nor even to produce policies which proclaim equality of opportunity, if the total ethos of a school does not support in every way a human rights perspective.

Thus, in teaching children to discover and live out their own identities among a variety of other identities, the solution is not to deny other identities but to seek ways of achieving harmony and cohesiveness amid diversity.

> The problem to be solved, therefore, is that of educating young children in a plural, diversified and heterogeneous society so as to favour the emergence of a firm and dynamic identity while enabling other identities to be accepted without demure. The solution is not to create identities of

a 'stronghold' kind and then attempt to educate them in open-mindedness but to reorganise plurality from the outset as an integral part of socialisation and acculturation. (Abdullah-Pretceille 1989 p.70)

Conclusion

The issue of children's rights is far more complex than some would have us believe. It is vitally important for children to be protected and to have their basic and educational and other needs met, but it is also important for them to be given real opportunities to become involved from an early age in decisions which affect them and others. Unless such opportunities are provided, or in Feuerstein's terms 'mediated', in homes and schools, children will not be prepared properly to exercise their rights to participation, to make choices, and ultimately, to contribute in a meaningful and constructive way to society.

Taking a rights perspective does not just mean meeting children's requirement or even their needs. There is a danger of overlooking the fact that exercising rights also involves accepting responsibilities. This message cannot be learned through an information transmission model of learning, but will ultimately depend upon an educational perspective which values and respects every person as both an individual and an integral member of society.

Such a perspective means in addition that it makes no sense to talk of special education as separate in some way from any other form of education. Questions are raised also about such terms as 'special educational needs'. Every school should by definition be providing something special in the form of education for all. Focusing upon the needs of one or another minority group or even upon the shifting needs of the majority may well lead, paradoxically, to a denial of their rights.

References

Abdullah-Pretceille, M. (1989) 'Human Rights in the Nursery School', in *The Challenge of Human Rights Education*. H. Stanley (ed.) London: Cassell.

Adelman, H. (1992) 'L.D. The Next 25 Years', in *Journal of Learning Disabilities* **25**, 17–22.

American Psychological Association (1995) 'Character education: popular but effective', in *APA Monitor* **March** 42–4.

Archard, D. (1993) *Children: Rights and Childhood*. London: Routledge.

Armstrong, D. (1995) *Power and Partnership in Education: Parents, Children and Special Educational Needs*. London: Routledge.

Armstrong, D., D. Galloway, S. Tomlinson (1993) 'Assessing special educational needs: the child's contribution', in *British Educational Research Journal* **19**, 121–31.

Atkinson, C. (1992) The Inner Lives of Asian Girls *unpublished M.Sc. thesis*. University of Sheffield.

Audit Commission and Her Majesty's Inspectors (1992) *Getting in on the Act*. London: HMSO.

Barnes, C. (1996) 'Theories of disability and the origin of oppression of disabled people in Western society', in *Disability and Society: Emerging Issues and Insights*, L. Barton (ed.) London: Longman.

Barnes, C., M. Oliver. (1995) 'Disability rights: rhetoric and reality in the UK', in *Disability and Society*, **10** 111–16.

Barrow, R. (1975) *Moral Philosophy for Education*. London: Allen and Unwin.

Barton, L., S. Tomlinson. (eds.) (1984) *Special Education And Social Interests*. London: Croom Helm

Bhogal, P. (1995) 'Parental Involvement in Secondary Schools', *unpublished M.Ed. dissertation*. University of Leeds.

Bless, G., C. Amrein (1992) 'The integration of pupils with learning difficulties: the results of research into the effects of integration', in *European Journal of Special Needs Education* **7**, 11–19.

Bolton, N. (1990) 'Educational psychology and the politics and practice of education', in *Refocusing Educational Psychology*, N. Jones, N.Frederickson (eds.), Lewes: Falmer Press.

Booth, T. (1996) 'Changing views of research on integration: the inclusion of students with 'special needs' or participation for all?, in *Psychology in Practice with Young People, Families and Schools*, A Sigston, P, Curran, A Labran and S, Wolfendale (eds.), London: David Fulton.

British Psychological Society, Division of Clinical Psychology (1994) *Guidelines for the Professional Practice of Clinical Psychology*, Leicester: British Psychological Society.

British Psychological Society, Division of Educational and Child Psychology (1994) *Guidelines for the Practice of Professional Educational Psychologists*, Leicester: British Psychological Society.

Bronfenbrenner, U. (1979) *The Ecology of Human Development: Experiments by Nature and Design*. Cambridge, MA: Harvard University Press.

Burden, R.L. (1992) 'Taking a human rights perspective', *School Psychology*

International **14**, (3), 195–98.

Butler, C. (1996) 'Mainstreaming experience in the United States: is it the appropriate educational placement for every disabled child?' *Developmental Medicine and Child Neurology*, **38**, 861–66.

Caesar, G. (1993) *Social Services for Black Children and Families*. London: National Children's Bureau.

Catholic Working Party on Multicultural Education (1984) *Learning from Diversity*. London: Catholic Media Office.

Choudhury, A. (1986) *Annual Report of Advisory Centre for Education*, London: ACE.

Clough, P., G. Lindsay (1991) *Integration and the Support Service*. Windsor: NFER-Nelson.

Coard, B. (1971) *How The West Indian Child is made Educationally sub-Normal in the British School System*. London: New Beacon Books.

Cole I., R. Furbey (1994) *The Eclipse Of Council Housing*. London: Routledge.

Cole, M. (1977) 'An ethnographic psychology of cognition', in *Thinking: Readings in Cognitive Science*, P. N. Johnson-Laird, P. C. Watson (eds.),Cambridge: Cambridge University Press.

Cole, T. (1989) *Apart or A Part? Integration and the Growth of British Special Education*. Milton Keynes: Open University Press.

Cooper, P. *et al.* (1991) 'Ethnic minority and gender distribution among staff and pupils in facilities for pupils with emotional and behavioural disorders in England and Wales', in *British Journal of Sociology of Education* **12**, 77–94.

Coopers and Lybrand (1992) *Within Reach: Access for Disabled Children to Mainstream School*. London: National Union of Teachers and Spastics Society.

Cordingley, P. and M. Kogan (1993) *In Support of Education*. London: Jessica Kingsley.

Cowne, E. and Norwich, B. (1987) *Lessons in Partnership. Bedford Way Paper 31*. London: Institute of Education.

Commission for Racial Equality (1988) *Learning in Terror*. London: Commission for Racial Equality.

Curriculum in the Primary School. London: Paul Chapman.

Damon, W. (1975) 'Early conceptions of positive justice as related to the development of logical operations', in *Child Development* **46**, 301–12.

Davie, R. (1993) 'Listen to the child: a time for change', in *The Psychologist*, **6**(6), 252–57.

Day, C., C. Hall, P. Gommage, and M. Coles (1993) *Leadership and Curriculum in the Primary School*. London: Paul Chapman.

DeBono, E. (1985) *Conflicts: A Better Way To Resolve Them*. London: Penguin Books.

Department of Education and Science (1978) *Special Educational Needs*. London: HMSO.

Department of Education and Science (1981) *West Indian Children in Our Schools*. London, HMSO.

Department of Education and Science (1985) *All Our Future*. London: HMSO.

Department of Education and Science (1989) *Discipline in Schools (The Elton Report)*. London: HMSO.

Department for Education (1992a) *Choice and Diversity*. London: Department for Education.

Department for Education (1992b) *Special Educational Needs: Access to the System*. London: Department for Education.

Department for Education (1994) *Code of Practice on the Identification and Assessment of Special Educational Needs*. London: HMSO.

Department for Education and Employment (1996) *School exclusion figures*. Bulletin 396/96. London: Department for Education and Employment.

Department of Health (1989) *An Introduction to the Children Act 1989*. London: HMSO.

Desforges, M. (1995) 'Assessment of special educational needs in bilingual pupils: Changing practice?' in *School Psychology International*, **16**, 5–17.

Desforges, M. and G. Lindsay (1995) 'Baseline Assessment'. in *Education and Child Psychology* **12**, 42–51.

Desforges, M., V. Mayet, and M. Vickers (1995) 'Psychological Assessment of Bilingual Children', in *Educational Psychology in Practice* **11**, 18–26.

Dunn, J. (1988) *The Beginnings of Social Understanding*. Oxford: Blackwell.

Dworkin, R. (1977) *Taking Rights Seriously*. London: Duckworth.

Emler, N. and J. Dickson (1993) 'The Child as Sociologist: the childhood development of implicit theories of role categories and social organisation', in *The Child as Psychologist: An introduction to the development of social cognition*, in M. Bennett (ed.). London: Harvester Wheatsheaf.

Eslea, M. and P.K. Smith (1994) *Anti-Bullying Work In Primary Schools*. Poster presented at the Annual Conference of the Developmental Section of the British Psychological Society, University of Portsmouth.

Feuerstein, R. and M. Hoffman (1982) 'Intergenerational conflict of rights: cultural imposition and self-realisation', in *Journal of School Psychology*, **58**, 14–63.

Fish, J. (1985) *Educational Opportunities for All?* London: Inner London Education Authority.

Fitzgibbon, C. (1996) *Monitoring Education: Indicators, Quality and Effectiveness*. London: Cassell.

Franklin, R. (1995) 'The case for children's rights: a progress report'. *The Handbook of Children's Rights*, in R. Franklin (ed.) London: Routledge.

Fulcher, G. (1989) *Disabling Policies: A Comparative Approach to Educational Policy and Disability*, London: Falmer Press.

Furze, T. and A. Conrad (1997) 'A review of parent partnership schemes', *Working with parents of SEN children after the Code of Practice*, S. Wolfendale (ed.), London: David Fulton.

Galloway, D. and C. Goodwin (1987) *The Education of Disturbing Children: Pupils with Learning and Adjustment Difficulties*. London: Longman.

Galloway, D., D. Armstrong and S. Tomlinson (1994) *Special Educational Needs: Whose Problem?* London: Longman.

Gash, H. and D. Coffey (1995) 'Influence on attitudes towards children with mental handicaps', in *European Journal of Special Educational Needs*, **10**, 1–16.

Gathorne-Hardy, J. (1977) *The Public School Phenomenon*. London: Hodder and Stoughton.

Gersch, I.S. (1992) 'Pupil involvement in assessment', *The Assessment of Special Educational Needs: International Perspectives*, in T.Cline (ed.), London: Routledge.

Gersch, I.S. (1996) 'Involving children in assessment: creating a listening ethos', in *Educational and Child Psychology*. **13**(2), 31–40.

Gersch, I.S., A. Holgate and A. Sigston (1993) 'Valuing the child's perspective: revised student report and other practical initiatives', in *Educational Psychology in Practice*, **9**(1), 36–45.

Gillborn, D. and C. Gipps (1996) *Recent Research on the Achievements of Ethnic Minority Pupils*. London: HMSO.

Gillham, W.E.C. (ed.) (1978) *Reconstructing Educational Psychology*. Beckenham: Croom Helm.

Goacher B., J. Evans, J. Welton and K. Wedell (1988) *Policy and provision for special educational needs. Implementing the 1981 Education Act*. London: Cassell.

Grant, D. and K. Brookes (1996) 'Exclusions from School – Responses from the Black Community', *Pastoral Care in Education* **14**, 20–27.

Gurnah, A. (1992) 'Sheffield Black Literacy Campaign', in *Adults Learning*, **3**, 196–200.

Hart, R. (1992) 'Children's Participation from Whenism to Citizenship', in *Innocenti Essays No.4*. London: UNICEF.

Hastings, R.P., E. Somuga-Barke, B. Remington (1993) 'An analysis of labels for people with learning disabilities', *British Journal of Clinical Psychology*, **32**, 463–65.

Hegarty, S (1993) *Meeting Special Needs in Ordinary Schools*. London: Cassell.

Herrnstein, R.J. and C. Murray (1994) *The Bell Curve*. London: Free Press.

Hewett, D. (1970) *The Family and the Handicapped Child*. London: Allen and Unwin.

Holmes, J. and R. Lindley (1991) *The Values of Psychotherapy*. Oxford: Oxford University Press.

Horton, T. (ed.) (1990) *Assessment Debates*. London: Hodder and Stoughton.

Hurt, J. S. (1988) *Outside the Mainstream*. London: Routledge.

Jarret, R. L. (1993) 'Voices from below: the value of ethnographic research for informing public policy', paper presented to the *Biennial Meeting of the Society for Research in Child Development*, New Orleans, March.

Jesson, D. (1996) *Value Added Measures of School GCSE Performance. Research Studies RS14*. London: Department for Education and Employment.

John, M. (1994) 'The UN Convention on the Rights of Child: development and implications', in *Educational and Child Psychology* **11**(4), 7–17.

Johnson, M. (1996) 'Models of disability', in *The Psychologist*, **9**, 205–10.

Jones, M. and R. Marchant (1993) 'A charter for children's rights', in *Educational and Child Psychology*, **10**(3), 60–62.

Katz, I. (1996) *Construction of Racial Identity in Children of mixed race parentage*. London: Jessica Kingsley.

Kohn, A. (1986) *No Contest: The Case Against Competition*. New York: Houghton Mifflen.

Lansdown, G. (1994) 'Monitoring the implementation of the UN Convention in the United Kingdom', in *Educational and Child Psychology*, **11**(4), 18–23.

Lawton, D. (1988) 'Ideologies of education', in T*he National Curriculum, Bedford Way Papers 33*, D. Lawton and C. Chitty (eds.). London: Institute of Education.

Lewis, A. and V. Lewis (1987). 'The attitudes of young children towards peers with severe learning difficulties', in *British Journal of Developmental Psychology*, **5**, 287–92.

Lewis, A. (1993) 'Primary school children's understanding of severe learning difficulties', in *Educational Psychology*, **13**, 133–45.

Lewis, A., S. Neill and J. Campbell (1997) 'SENCOs and the Code: a national survey', in *Support for Learning*, **12**, 3–9.

Lindsay, G (1989) 'Evaluating integration', in *Educational Psychology in Practice*, **5**, 7–16.

Lindsay G. (1995) 'Values, ethics and psychology', in *The Psychologist*, **8**,(11), 493–98

Lindsay, G, and M. Desforges (1986) 'Integrated nurseries for children with special educational needs', in *British Journal of Special Education*, **13**, 63–66.

Lindsay, G. and D. Dickinson (1987) 'The integration of profoundly hearing impaired children into a nursery setting', in *Journal of the British Association of Teachers of the Deaf*, **11**, 1–7.

Lindsay, G. (1995a) 'Early identification of special educational needs, in *Psychology and Education for Special Needs*, I. Lunt and B. Norwich (eds.), London: Arena, Ashgate.

Lindsay, G. (1996) 'Children with special educational needs: some ethical issue for practitioners in the UK', in *International Journal of Practical Approaches to Disability*, **20**, 12–18.

Lindsay, G. and A. Colley (1995) 'Ethical dilemmas of members of the Society', in *The Psychologist*, **8**, 214—17.

Lindsay, G., R. Quayle, G. Lewis and C. Jessop (1990) *Special Educational Needs Review 1990*, Sheffield: Local Education Authority.

Lipsky, M. (1980) *Street-Level Bureaucrats*. New York: Russell Sage.

Mac an Ghiall, M. (1989) 'Coming of Age in 1980s' England: reconceptualising Black students' schooling experience', in *British Journal of Sociology of Education*, **10**, 273–86.

Madden, N. A. and R. E. Slavin (1983) 'Mainstreaming students with mild handicaps: academic and social outcomes', in *Review of Educational Research*, **53**, 519—69.

Madge, N. and M. Fassam (1982). *Ask the Children*. London: Batsford Academic and Educational.

Martlew, M. and J. Hodson (1991) 'Children with mild learning difficulties in an integrated and in a special school: comparison of behaviour, teasing and teachers' attitudes', in *British Journal of Educational Psychology*, **61**, 355–72.

Masson, J. (1990) *The Children Act 1989: Text and Commentary*. London: Sweet and Maxwell.

McConkey, R. (1985) *Working with Parents: A practical guide for teachers and therapists*. London: Croom Helm.

McIntyre, K. (1995) 'Pastoral Care and Black Pupils', *Children with Emotional and Behavioural Difficulties*. P. Farrell. (ed.). London: Falmer Press.

Meighan, R. (1990) 'Alternative roles for learners with particular reference on learner as democratic explorer in teacher education courses', in *The School Field*, **1**,(1), 61—77.

Montgomery, G. (ed.) (1981) *The Integration and Disintegration of the Deaf in Society*. Edinburgh: Scottish Workshop for the Deaf.

Morton, J. (1996) 'Helping children contribute to learning plans', in *Educational and Child Psychology* **13**,(2), 23–30.

Murray-Seegert, C. (1989) *Nasty Girls, Thugs and Humans Like Us: Social Relations Between Severely Disabled and Non-Disabled Students in High School*. Baltimore: Brookes.

National Curriculum Council (1989) *A Curriculum For All* York: National Curriculum Council.

Newham Council (undated) *Strategy for Inclusive Education 1996–2001*. London: Newham Council.

Newnes C. (1996) 'The development of clinical psychology and its values', in *Clinical Psychology Forum* **95**.

Ng, K. (1992) 'An Investigation into Chinese Parents' perceptions of their children's special educational needs', *M.Sc. thesis*, University of Sheffield.

Norwich, B. (1994) 'Differentiation: from the perspective of resolving tensions between basic social values and assumptions about individual differences', *Curriculum Studies* **2**, 289–308.

Norwich, B. (1996) 'Special needs education or education for all: connective specialisation and ideological impurity, in *British Journal of Special Education* **23**, 100–103.

Nunes, T. (1994) 'The environment of the child', in *International Journal of Early Years Education*, **2**, 3–37.

Office for Standards in Education (1996) *The Teaching of Reading in 45 Inner London Primary Schools*. London: OFSTED (Ref: 27/96/DS).

Office of Her Majesty's Chief Inspector of Schools (1996a) *Exclusions from Secondary Schools 1995–96*. London: The Stationery Office.

Office of Her Majesty's Chief Inspector of Schools (1996b) *Subjects And Standards: Issues for School Development Arising From OFSTED Inspection Findings 1994–5. Key Stage 1 and 2*. London: HMSO.

Office of Her Majesty's Chief Inspector of Schools (1996c) *Promoting High Achievement for Pupils with Special Educational Needs in Mainstream Schools*. London: HMSO.

Oliver, M. (1992) 'Intellectual masturbation: a rejoinder to Soder and Booth', *European Journal of Special Education*, **7**, 20–28.

Olomolaiye, F. (1995) 'Experiences of a Black Psychologist', unpublished manuscript, Sheffield: Local Education Authority, Psychological Service.

Ormell, C. (1980) 'Values in Education', in R. Straughton and J.Wrigley (eds.), *Values and Evaluation in Education*, London: Harper and Row.

Osborne, E. (1994) 'The child, the family and the school' in *The Family and the*

School, E. Dowling, and E. Osborne (eds.). (2nd edn.) London, New York: Routledge.

Parfitt, G. (1996) 'School student self assessment and appraisal', *internal report of work in progress*, University of Exeter: School of Education.

Peter, M. (1995) 'Lobbying for special education', in *Psychology and Education for Special Needs*, I. Lunt and B. Norwich (eds.). London: Arena, Ashgate.

Pfeiffer, D. (1994) 'Eugenics and disability discrimination', in *Disability and Society*, **9**, 481–99.

Phillips, M. (1997) *All Must Have Prizes*. London: Little Brown.

Pumfrey, P. (1996) 'Specific developmental dyslexia: Basics to Back'. *Vernon-Wall lecture*, Leicester: British Psychological Society.

'Racial harassment in School', in *Highlight 92*. London: National Children's Bureau.

Ramasut, A. (1989) *Whole School Approaches to Special Needs*. London, New York: Falmer Press.

Ratchfurd, D. and H.G. Furth (1986) 'Understanding of friendship and social rules in deaf and hearing adolescents', in *Journal of Applied Developmental Psychology*, **7**, 391–402.

Raven, J. (1988) 'Equity in Diversity: The problems posed by values and their resolution', in *Parents and schools: The contemporary challenge*, P. MacCleod (ed.). London: Falmer Press.

Ravenette, T. (1980) 'The exploration of consciousness: personal construct intervention with children', in *Personal Construct Psychology: Psychotherapy and Personality*, A.W. Landfield, L.M. Leitner (eds.). London: J. Wiley.

Rehal, A. (1989) 'Involving Asian Parents in the statementing procedure – the way forward', *Educational Psychology in Practice*, **4**, 189–97.

Riddick, B. (1995).'Dyslexia', in *Disability and Society*, **10**, 457–73.

Romaine, S. (1994) *Bilingualism*, London: Blackwell.

Rosenbaum, M. and P. Newell (1991) *Taking Children Seriously: A Proposal For A Children's Rights Commissioner*. London: Gulbenkian Foundation.

Safran, S. (1995) 'Peers' perceptions of emotional and behavioural disorders: What are students thinking?', in *Journal of Emotional and Behavioural Disorders* 3, 66–75.

Sale, P. and D. M. Carey (1995) 'The sociometric status of students with disabilities in a full-inclusion school', *Exceptional Children* **62**, 6–19.

Salisbury, C. L., C. Gallucci, M. Palombaro and C. A. Peck (1995) 'Strategies that promote social relations among elementary students with and without severe disabilities in inclusive schools', in *Exceptional Children*, **62**, 125–37.

Sameroff, A.J., M.J. Chandler (1975) 'Reproductive risk and the continuum of caretaking casualty', in *Review of child development research*, F.D. Horowitz (ed.), **4**, 187–244. Chicago: University of Chicago Press.

Schön, D.A. (1983) *The Reflective Practitioner: How Professionals Think in Action*. London: Temple Smith.

School Curriculum and Assessment Authority (1996) Equity in diversity: the Problems Posed by Values and their Resolution. London: SCAA Publications.

Scruggs, T. E. and M. A. Mastropieri (1996) 'Teacher perceptions of mainstreaming inclusion 1958–1995: a recent synthesis', in *Exceptional Children*, **63**, 59–74.

Sharp, S., D.A. Thompson (1994) 'The Role Of Whole School Policies In Tackling Bullying Behaviour In Schools', *School Bullying: Insights And Perspectives*, P.K. Smith and S. Sharp (eds.), London: Routledge.

Simmons, K. (1996) 'In defence of entitlement', in *Support for Learning*, **11**,(3), 105–108.

Skrtic, T. M. (1991) *Behind Special Education*. Colorado: Love.

Sloper, P., C. Cunningham, S. Turner and C. Knussen (1990) 'Factors related to the academic attainments of children with Down's Syndrome', in *British Journal of Educational Psychology*, **60**, 284–98.

Smetana, J.G., M. Kelly and C.T. Twentyman (1984) 'Abused, neglected and nonmaltreated children's conceptions of moral and conventional transgressions', in *Child Development*, **55**, 277–87.

Smith, P.K. and S. Sharp (eds.) (1994) *School Bullying: Insights And Perspectives*.

London: Routledge.

Spencer, N. (1996) *Poverty and Child Health*. Oxford: Radcliffe Medical Press.

Sheffield Unified Multicultural Education Service (1993) *Sumes Review Report*. Sheffield: Local Education Authority.

Thompson, D.A. (1995) *Two Years On: Problems In Monitoring Anti-Bullying Policies In Schools And Their Effects On The Incidence Of Bullying*. Paper presented at the European Conference on Educational Research, 14—17 September 1995, University of Bath.

Thompson, D.A. and S. Sharp (1994) *Improving Schools: Integrating Whole School Behaviour Policies*. London: David Fulton.

Tomlinson, S. (1980) 'Ethnic Minority Parents and education'. in *Linking home and school*, M. Craft *et al.* (eds.), London: Harper Row.

Tomlinson, S. (1982) *A Sociology of Special Education*. London: Routledge.

Tomlinson, S. (1988) 'Why Johnny can't read: critical theory and special education', in *European Journal of Special Needs Education* **3**, 45–58.

Tomlinson, S. (1989) 'Education and Training', in *New Community* **15**. 461–69.

Tomlinson, S. (1994) 'The Assessment of Special Educational Needs: Whose Problem?' in *Special Educational Needs: Whose Problem?* D. Galloway, *et al.* London: Longmans.

Torrington, D. and J. Weightman (1989) *The Reality of School Management*. Oxford: Blackwell.

Troyna, B. (1981) *Public Awareness and the Media: A study reporting on Race*, London: Community Relations Commission.

Troyna, B. (1993) *Racism and Education*. Buckingham: Open University Press.

Troyna, B. and B. Carrington (1990) *Education, Racism and Reform*. London: Routledge.

Tyson, S. and T. Jackson (1992) *The Essence Of Organisational Behaviour*. Hemel Hempstead: Prentice Hall.

Vincent C., J. Evans, I. Lunt, P. Young (1996) 'Professionals under Pressure: the administration of special education in a changing context', in *British Educational Research Journal*, **22**, (4), 475–92

Wade, B. and M. Moore (1993) *Experiencing Special Education*. Buckingham: Open University Press.

Watts, J. (1989) 'Up To A Point', *The Democratic School: Educational Management And The Practice Of Democracy*, C. Harber and R. Meighan (eds.), Ticknall: Education Now.

Wedell, K. and G. Lindsay (1980) 'Early identification procedures: What have we learned?' in *Remedial Education* **15**, 130–35.

Wilding, P. (1982) *Professional Power and Social Welfare*. London: Routledge.

Wolfendale, S. (1987) *Special Needs in Ordinary Schools*. London: Cassell.

Wright, C. (1986) 'School Processes – An Ethnographic Study', in *Education for Some*, J. Eggleston *et al.* (eds) Stoke-on-Trent: Trentham Books.

Yoshida, R.K., L. Wasilewski and D. L. Friedman (1990) 'Recent newspaper coverage about persons with disabilities', *Exceptional Children* **56**, 5.

Index